Plays
by
Daniel Damiano
Volume 2
(Short Plays)

Cut

The Art of Tea

Spell

The Dessert Cart

The Lepers

Stay

The King of Something

A Moment of Weakness

The Survey

A Lesson in Captivity

The Enlightenment of Mrs. Cartwell

Did You Hear the One About the Mexican Laundress?

Production Photo Credits (from Top, and l-r):
Cut – WorkShop Theater Company, NYC, 2011 - World Premier   (Pictured l-r,
Jonathan Weber and Ken Glickfeld)
The Enlightenment of Mrs. Cartwell, Estrogenius Festival, NYC, 2009 - NYC Prem-
ier, Photographed by Nichole Donje' (Pictured l-r, Anna Emily Altman, Mia
Moreland, Laura Piquado and Annalisa Loeffler)
The Lepers, Ensemble Studio Theatre, NYC, 2019 – World Premier
Photographed by Jeremy Daniel (Pictured l-r, Wilma Rivera and Joseph Cassese)
The Dessert Cart – fandango 4 productions and Mind The Gap Theatre Company,
NYC, 2011 – NYC Revival (Pictured l-r, Emma Gordon, Justin Herfel, Simon Pearl
and Stuart Williams)
A Moment of Weakness – fandango 4 productions and Mind The Gap Theatre Compa-
ny, NYC, 2011 – NYC Revival (Pictured l-r, Sue Glausen and Judy Alvarez)
Spell - Algonquin Theatre Company, NYC, 2008 – World Premier (Pictured l-r,
Michael Janove and Kathryn Kates)
Stay - fandango 4 productions and Mind The Gap Theatre Company, NYC, 2011 –
NYC Revival (Pictured l-r, George Stavropoulos and DH Johnson)
The Art of Tea - fandango 4 productions and Mind The Gap Theatre Company, NYC,
2011 – World Premier (Pictured l-r, Kate Greer and Anna Emily Altman)
Did You Hear the One About the Mexican Laundress? - Howling Moon Cab Compa-
ny, NYC, 2008, NYC Premier. (Pictured l-r, Judy Alvarez, Andrew Dahl and
Nicholas Daniele)
The Survey – Studio Theater in Exile, Peekskill, NY, 2025, World Premier (Pictured
l-r, Basia Zak and Joan Cavallo)

Praise for the Plays

CUT

(2011 Arts & Letters Prize Finalist)
""...a fascinating character study..."
Steve Allen, Stage Door St. Louis

"Damiano puts well the barber's lessons and losses."
Bob Wilcox, HEC-TV, St. Louis

THE ART OF TEA

"This Wildean-inspired comedy of manners was a joy to watch
and the perfect way to end the first half of the evening."
Michael Davis, Female Arts (UK)

"Four Stars - Damiano takes a loving pot-shot at British
sensibilities creating a comic piece of nuance and intrigue."
GrumpyGayCritic (UK)

THE DESSERT CART

(2024 David A. Einhorn Playwriting Prize)
"…the evening's best and most surprising. The play ripens into
a surreal exploration of the different ways people define
satisfaction, and the toll taken by our convergent definitions."
Jeffrey Lewonczyk, nytheatre.com

DID YOU HEAR THE ONE ABOUT
THE MEXICAN LAUNDRESS?

"It's refreshing to expose excesses of the Department of Homeland
Security through satire.- The play is Kafka-meets-the-Keystone-
Kops and it's another high point of the festival."
Lydia Howell, Pulse of the Twin Cities

I had the great pleasure of directing a few of these pieces in their earliest productions, and it was wonderful to revisit them in this remarkably diverse collection, as well as the other pieces which I was not as familiar with. For a director, there's a real magic in being part of a play's first staging—seeing a script come to life and discovering how it lands with an audience. Even more special was the opportunity to collaborate directly with Daniel on a number of these productions. His openness, sense of humor, and deep respect for the craft made the process not only creatively fulfilling, but genuinely fun.

Therefore, it's a real joy for me to introduce this collection of short plays — each one a distinct gem, offering its own rhythm, voice, and spark. What unites them is variety: in tone, style, and the wonderful range of characters they bring to life. Some of these pieces lean into the absurd with wild, unexpected turns; others are more grounded and naturalistic, quietly revealing emotional depth and nuance. That blend keeps the collection vibrant, surprising, and deeply human, in addition to being a gift for actors looking to inhabit rich, layered characters.

Supporting new writing for the stage is essential if we want theatre to stay bold, relevant, and reflective of the world we live in. Daniel Damiano's work reminds us just how exciting new voices can be—original, thoughtful, and always engaging. I hope this collection sparks new productions, fresh conversations, and the kind of creative energy that live theatre thrives on.

- *Paula D'Alessandris*
Theatre Director/Artistic Director
Mind The Gap Theatre Company, NYC

A WORD FROM A PLAYWRIGHT

As many in the Theatre world know, plays in the short form, while perhaps easier to find productions in the seemingly endless array of one-act festivals that remain ubiquitous, are also subject to fading into the ether of a playwright's career due to their sheer brevity.

With that often being the case, it's particularly satisfying for me to have some of my short work preserved here in a collection that I'm, dare I say, quite proud of.   In revisiting and assembling these plays from the last 25 years of my playwriting career, it is telling how many of the themes remain relevant to today. And in some cases, sadly so – an example being 2007's *Did You Hear the One About the Mexican Laundress?*, an absurdist take on the abduction of a legal immigrant by federal agents. In re-reading these plays, some for the first time in a while, I also found it particularly moving to recall various line readings from the many fine actors who've played these roles over the years, and am equally thrilled to include in this collection the many performers and directors who helped bring these plays to life.

All that said, to anyone who has come upon these plays simply as a curious reader, I thank you for your curiosity.

And to the artist in any field who feels cast aside or that their talent and passion have been rendered insignificant by the absence of mass acknowledgement and adoration, please know that you are a success still – for all who seek to create and share their soulful creations with the world *are*. Especially now.

-   *Daniel Damiano*
4/5/25

Plays

CUT

CUT

CUT received its World Premiere as part of the WorkShop Theater Company's Cold Snaps Festival, December 2011, in New York City, with the following cast and director:

RAYMOND…………………..Jonathan Weber

JERRY……………………...…Ken Glickfeld

Directed by Paula D'Alessandris

Artistic Director: Scott Sickles

CUT was subsequently revived as part of the 1st Annual Neil Labute New Theater Festival, July 2013, produced by St. Louis Actors' Studio at the Gaslight Theatre in St. Louis, MO, with David Wassilak as Jerry and Tom Lehman as Raymond. Directed by Steve Woolf

Cast of Characters

RAYMOND – *30's. Well-built, from Queens, NY. An inmate. Struggling to find the balance between the lawlessness of prison-life and his ambitions to change himself and broaden his intellect.*

JERRY – *60's, from Brooklyn, NY. A prison barber, as well as an inmate. Has been imprisoned for almost 30 years and, over that time, has established himself as somewhat of an old sage.*

A maximum-security prison barber shop.

The time is the present.

JERRY is currently trimming RAYMOND, who sits in chair.
They are in the midst of a discussion…

RAYMOND: It don't mean it ain't true.

JERRY: It's an excuse.

RAYMOND: Yeah, but it's a *real* excuse.

JERRY: No, it ain't.

RAYMOND: Joe, c'mon…

JERRY: It's called *rationalization*, Ray, plain'n simple.

RAYMOND: What?

JERRY: Y'gonna' tell me you don't know what *that* is now?

RAYMOND: No, I know...

JERRY: Well, there y'go.

RAYMOND: Y'sayin' it's an excuse.

JERRY: Don't move so much.

RAYMOND: *(Looks ahead...)* You're not gonna' tell me we don't come from somethin'.

JERRY: I'm not tellin' y'that. 'Course we come from… Keep your head still.

RAYMOND: Sorry.

JERRY: 'Course we come from somethin'. But you're talkin' Jung, and it don't apply here.

RAYMOND: Talkin' what?

JERRY: How you're raised contributes to a personality, which is what *he* said.

RAYMOND: I don't even know who you're talkin' about. Yoon?

JERRY: *Jung.*

RAYMOND: What, he Chinese or somethin'?

JERRY: He's Swedish, but that's beside the point. A personality is not an action, y'see what I'm sayin'?

RAYMOND: But, wait, Jer, your personality contributes to what you do, right…?

JERRY: Apples'n oranges…

RAYMOND: C'mon…

JERRY: Two different things, Ray. n'anybody who tells ya' differently is talkin' outa' their ass.

RAYMOND: *(Digests this.)* Shit, then I guess I'll be tiltin' my ears next time I'm meetin' with the shrink, 'cause that's what he's sayin'.

JERRY: He's a shrink, Ray. He ain't God.

RAYMOND: So he's fulla' shit?

JERRY: Look, I don't know the guy enough to know what he's fulla', okay? He seems like a nice enough guy, educated'n all that shit. n'I've had a few interesting chats with those types t'not make a blanket statement,…but it don't change the funda-mentals.

RAYMOND: n'what are those?

JERRY: The facts.

RAYMOND: n'what are *those*?

(JERRY stops trimming.)

JERRY: Alright, lemme phrase it like this; I can name the names of at least a dozen white collar dudes who came from the most pristine upbringings, right?

RAYMOND: Alright.

JERRY: I'm talkin' like *Great Gatsby* shit, okay? Rich father, rich mother, a dog, a cat, horses… They got everything they wanted from them; money, cars, all that shit, right?

RAYMOND: Alright.

JERRY: Alright?

RAYMOND: Yeah.

JERRY: They went to Ivy League colleges, graduated with this'n that from what'n what, right?

RAYMOND: Yeah.

JERRY: They married their childhood sweethearts, had 2.3 kids, got a beautiful home with the dog'n the white picket fence, tomato garden'n all…

RAYMOND: Alright.

JERRY: Right?

RAYMOND: Yeah, tomatoes, white fence…

JERRY: Then one lovely day, this walkin' American Cream Dream takes a newly purchased magnum and shoots his beautiful wife point blank in the temple.

RAYMOND: Okay, but…

JERRY: Not only that, wait… He saws her limbs off, throws everything in a bag, throws the bag in the trunk, brings her out to a place that he *thinks* clears him but, nonetheless, is a place she can be found. Because, of course, if she's *found*, she's confirmed dead which means he can collect the insurance that he can lavish on the stripper he's been pokin' for 3 years. Okay?

RAYMOND: But, Jer…

JERRY: Wait. Now, you're gonna' tell me that this action stemmed from his upbringing? I mean, shit, he may've been a little yuppy snot and thought his shit didn't stink, but his parents sure as fuck didn't put him up to *this*. So what were the real roots of his actions?

RAYMOND: *(A beat.)* Greed.

JERRY: You're fuckin' A right.. One of the 3 reasons why someone becomes a criminal, regardless of education, regardless of wealth; greed, desperation & rage. Whatever we fall under is what we fall under, Ray,…but that don't change what we did.

RAYMOND: Okay, but…

JERRY: So the point I'm makin' is a *lota'* guys asses've been kicked by their fathers. You can blame your father for kickin' your ass all you want,…but ya' did what ya' did. *(A beat.)* And you don't deny what ya' did, right?

RAYMOND: *(Slight pause, slightly humbled.)* No, I… I know what I did.

JERRY: Alright then. These are strides y'makin'.

(JERRY resumes trimming, as RAYMOND absorbs this, begrudgingly…)

RAYMOND: But my father *was* a shit, Jerry.

JERRY: But y'understand what I'm sayin'.

RAYMOND: Yeah, I got ya'…

JERRY: Y'understand?

RAYMOND: Yeah, no one forced me…

JERRY: Right. Y'gotta' take responsibility. The day you come to terms with that is the day you'll make headway with that parole board. But you choose t'live in the past, n'blamin' your father'n mother n'the Holy Ghost, they don't got reason to think that you'll ever get past it. And they'll suspect you'll jus' fuck up again the moment they let you out.

RAYMOND: Yeah.

JERRY: Rationalization ain't gonna' do you shit.

RAYMOND: Yeah, okay…

JERRY: But fuck that, man. You gotta' believe it *yourself.* *That's* what this is about. It's about your own growth.

RAYMOND: Yeah, I hear ya'…

JERRY: It's about decontaminatin' your mind, not about auditioning for them.

RAYMOND: Yeah,...

JERRY: This ain't *American Idol*, f'Godsakes.

RAYMOND: Okay.

JERRY: You be true t' yourself, n'they'll see it. Unless they're fuckin' idiots. But they'll see it. So that's what y'work towards.

(JERRY resumes trimming. A moment.)

RAYMOND: I dunno', Jer.

JERRY: What don't y'know?

RAYMOND: They jus' denied me.

JERRY: Of course, they did. You weren't ready.

RAYMOND: *(Internally.)* My soul is fuckin' dyin' in here.

JERRY: Ray, they don't give a shit about that. This is what the hell we're talkin' about here. The outside world don't need another dyin' man. You gotta' survive as good as you can in here in order t'live out there, y'hear me? That means y'can't be fuckin' around.

RAYMOND: I *am* survivin'. I'm here, right?

JERRY: But you're doin' it at the expense of havin' your rep tarnished.

RAYMOND: My rep...?

JERRY: I'm not talkin' about your *prisoner*-rep. I'm talkin' about what gets reported. What the guards see, what the parole board sees… You gotta' watch who you're hangin' with.

RAYMOND: It's either hang with 'em or be their prey, Jer…

JERRY: Listen t'me…

RAYMOND: Shit, I'm not like you, man. I'm not a…a beacon a' wisdom. Guys respect you.

JERRY: You think that happened overnight?

RAYMOND: No, but I'm jus' sayin', they respect you. They sit in here, you make 'em laugh, you give 'em things to think about… Who am I, man? So I gotta' bust heads sometimes.

JERRY: Look, I tussled in my first coupla' years. Okay? But I was *defendin'* myself. You can defend yourself, Ray,…but you shouldn't be the aggressor jus' cause you're a big drink a' water.

RAYMOND: *(Slight pause, slightly defensive.)* Who says I'm the agressor?

JERRY: You think I jus' fell off a Goddamn turnip truck? You think info isn't circulated around here?

RAYMOND: It can be bullshit too.

JERRY: Is it?

> *(RAYMOND does not respond, before JERRY resumes trimming.)*

Jus' cause you're in a box don't mean y'can't think outside it. I told ya' before, they got books here. Read 'em. Y'think I knew shit when I got here? Y'think I knew how t'fuckin' cut hair? I coulda' been a toughy'n done nothin' but act tough. But I read, I watched, I trained. I developed a little wisdom in the process. But these guys, they sit in my chair'n they act like they hear me, and then they walk out the door'n do the same shit. No desire t'be anything other than what they think they are. Those're the guys who'll never see the light a' day. You wana' be like them? Fine. You'll be comin' here for haircuts the resta' your life.

RAYMOND: Jer, I'm not gonna' argue with ya', okay? I'm jus' sayin, there's a reality that I deal with that maybe you never had to….

JERRY: *(Over "never had to…")* **Don't gimme that shit**! I been here almost 30 Goddamn years n'I ain't ever gettin' out. I will never step on grass again, y'understand? I will never have real New York pizza again. I'll never be with a woman again. You talkin' t'me about fuckin' **reality**?!

> *(A moment, before JERRY resumes trimming, a little slower now; pensively.)*

RAYMOND: *(Appeasing, somewhat…)* I been goin' to the Library.

JERRY: I thought you were bustin' heads.

RAYMOND: I'm not around 'em all the time. I get away. I looked at some a' the books you recommended.

JERRY: *(Skeptical.)* Oh, yeah?

RAYMOND: Yeah.

JERRY: Does "looked" mean *actually read*?

RAYMOND: Some, yeah…

JERRY: *House of the Dead*?

RAYMOND: What?

JERRY: You read *House of the Dead* yet?

RAYMOND: Yeah, I….

13

JERRY: You *read* it?

RAYMOND: The back, yeah.

JERRY: Oh, gimme a fuckin'...

RAYMOND: *(Snickers, over "gimme a fuckin'...)* What, Jer? I'm in prison already and you're givin' me a book about a guy in a Siberian prison camp?

JERRY: It's about his spiritual awakening. How he overcomes his surroundings.

RAYMOND: I know the surroundings.

JERRY: He got out!

RAYMOND: Well, good for him.

JERRY: *(A beat, offended.)* I tell you what, how about I don't talk from here on out.

RAYMOND: Jerry, c'mon...

JERRY: No, really, I'll jus' save my tongue, okay? You come for your monthly haircut and I'll just shut up. What the fuck's the point?

> *(A moment. RAYMOND is offguarded by JERRY's display. JERRY is still.)*

RAYMOND: Jer,...what's up with you today. You alright?

JERRY: *(A beat. Bitterly.)* I dunno', must be the day.

RAYMOND: What's the day? What happened?

JERRY: *(A beat.)* Don't worry about it.

> *(JERRY resumes cutting. A moment.)*

RAYMOND: I get somethin' from this, man. Believe it or not. You get the…the fuckin' blood goin' to my brain. Don't get all pissed. It's jus' when I'm out there, I feel like I gotta'… If I lower my guard…

(JERRY abruptly finishes . He takes a mirror, as if without thinking, and positions it behind RAYMOND's head. RAYMOND hesitantly nods approvingly.)

(JERRY places mirror back, brushes off RAYMOND's shoulders…)

RAYMOND: We done?

(As JERRY removes hair cloth from RAYMOND…)

JERRY: *(A beat.)* Yeah, we're done. Unless you want the goat trimmed too.

RAYMOND: No, it's cool. I like it like this.

JERRY: Of course y'do. Y'look like the fuckin' Devil.

(RAYMOND laughs, JERRY reluctantly smirks, but remains unusually distracted… RAYMOND rises, brushes the excess hair off…)

JERRY: *(Without making eye contact…)* I have a son, y'know.

RAYMOND: *(A beat.)* I didn't know that.

JERRY *(A beat.)* His birthday's t'day.

RAYMOND: *(A beat.)* Shit, y'serious? T'day?

JERRY: *(Slight pause, with some difficulty.)* Mm. A little older than you. But anyway,…he's out there somewhere. He was around 6 or so when I got in here, but he didn't know much about me then either. He's never visited. I don't want 'im too. This is *my* penance, not his, y'know? *(Slight pause, with irony.)* A fuckin' doctor. Cardiologist. My sista' sent me letters when

15

she was alive. She was my only connection t'him. *(Slight pause.)* Sometimes...I thinka' the conversations he must have. High School reunions, people askin' him how he became so successful. Who inspired him. And he's sayin', "Not my father, I'll tell ya' that much. - *He* was a shit."

(A moment. JERRY lifts his shameful head and makes eye contact with RAYMOND, who is somewhat embarrassed.)

You can have 'im send the next guy in.

(JERRY sweeps around chair, as RAYMOND observes him, awkwardly.)

(RAYMOND then looks toward entryway, takes a few steps towards it. Rolls up his sleeves to reveal a few ominous tattoos, toughens his veneer. It is as if he has transformed before our eyes.)

RAYMOND: *(Curtly.)* See ya'.

(RAYMOND exits, as JERRY slowly sweeps, appearing to age before us.)

(Lights fade.)

End of Play

THE ART OF TEA

THE ART OF TEA

The Art of Tea received its World Premiere as part of *The World is My Cheesecake,* an Evening of One-Act plays by Daniel Damiano, produced by Mind The Gap Theatre Company and fandango 4 productions, September 2011, in New York City, with the following cast and director:

ANNABELL……………..……Anna Emily Altman
CYNTHIA………...……………….....Kate Greer

Directed by Paula D'Alessandris

Artistic Directors:
Paula D'Alessandris (Mind The Gap)
Daniel Damiano & Judy Alvarez (fandango 4 productions)

The Art of Tea was subsequently revived as part Encompass Productions' Bare Essentials Short Play Festival, October 2014, at the Take Courage Theatre in London, England, with Laurie Harrington as Cynthia and Carly Halse as Annabell. Directed by Rachael Owens

Cast of Characters

ANNABELL – *A woman in her late 30's, early 40's. British.*

CYNTHIA – *A woman in her late 30's, early 40's. British.*

Cynthia's terrace outside of her apartment in London.

The Time is the Present.

ANNABELL & CYNTHIA sit at a small circular table,
having tea, smiling.

ANNABELL: Well, this is certainly very nice.

CYNTHIA: Oh, well, it's only English Breakfast.

ANNABELL: No, I mean,…being here.

CYNTHIA: Oh, well, it's my pleasure.

ANNABELL: I have to say that I'm more than a bit surprised.

CYNTHIA: By what?

ANNABELL: Well, you having me over.

CYNTHIA: Why would that surprise you?

ANNABELL: Well, I mean,…considering.

CYNTHIA: Considering what?

ANNABELL: Well, I mean…considering…what's happened.

CYNTHIA: What's happened?

ANNABELL: Well,…between us.

CYNTHIA: Well, dear, everyone has their differences, yes? It's simply the natural course of things.

ANNABELL: Yes, well,…maybe.

CYNTHIA: Of course.

ANNABELL: It's just that…these…differences have been a bit more…considerable, yes?

CYNTHIA: What do you mean?

ANNABELL: Between us?

CYNTHIA: Why?

ANNABELL: Considering.

CYNTHIA: Considering what?

ANNABELL: Considering that I...

CYNTHIA: Yes?

ANNABELL: We...

CYNTHIA: Yes?

ANNABELL: You...

CYNTHIA: Yes?

ANNABELL: ...found me in bed with your husband.

CYNTHIA: *(A beat, recalling.)* Oh, yes, I suppose I did.

ANNABELL: Just 2 weeks ago.

CYNTHIA: Yes.

ANNABELL: In...your own bed.

CYNTHIA: Yes. I recall now.

ANNABELL: You were rather upset.

CYNTHIA: Well, I suppose I must've been, yes?

ANNABELL: Justifiably so, of course.

CYNTHIA: *(Slight pause.)* Of course, in fairness, those aren't really *differences*.

ANNABELL: I'm sorry?

CYNTHIA: You sleeping with Robert. It's not a *difference*. You were having sexual relations with him and I witnessed it, so actually we're in complete agreement about that, yes?

ANNABELL: Yes, I…I suppose we are.

CYNTHIA: You're not disputing that.

ANNABELL: No.

CYNTHIA: There you were.

ANNABELL: Yes.

CYNTHIA: There he was.

ANNABELL: Yes.

CYNTHIA: There you both were.

>   *(A moment, as they gaze out. CYNTHIA sips her tea, pensively. ANNABELL awkwardly observes…)*

ANNABELL: Of course, I apologized.

CYNTHIA: Oh, did you.

ANNABELL: Yes. Extensively.

CYNTHIA: That must be why I've made you tea.

ANNABELL: *(Slight pause.)* Well, I mean, normally, an apology wouldn't be considered enough.

CYNTHIA: Why is that?

ANNABELL: Well, I mean,…considering.

CYNTHIA: Ah, yes, considering the boot-knocking with my significant other.

ANNABELL: Well, for lack of a better term.

CYNTHIA: Oh, I'm sorry. Was I being too crude in my description of your sexual foray with my husband?

ANNABELL: Well, I…

CYNTHIA: Should I have been more refined about it?

ANNABELL: Um, well…

CYNTHIA: Your bump-and-grind session?

ANNABELL: That's…

CYNTHIA: Your ass-probing conference?

ANNABELL: I think…

CYNTHIA: Your shagadagadingdonging!

ANNABELL: Alright, Cynthia, that's quite enough!

CYNTHIA: *(Rises, hostilely…)* No, I must agree with you, Annabell.

ANNABELL: What?

CYNTHIA: Your apology. It's **not** enough! It was an error in judgment. **My** judgment, which has only served to repress my memory. I should've known better than to invite you over for tea, but I tried to remain loyal to my roots. Yet, what I've learned today is that roots often belie the soil.

ANNABELL: I don't know what that means.

CYNTHIA: *(With building intensity…)* When my mother was young, she had recalled a story that her mother had told her that her mother had told her that her mother had told her. My multiple-greatgrandmother was a prisoner of a type of war in some type of country somewhere. She was abducted by enemy troops and forced to carry the artillery and food of a dozen soldiers who walked freely for miles; laughing, joking, taunting her every step until she collapsed. She would wake up hours later only to discover that the entire battalion had been killed, or at least she had thought. She ran alone for miles until rescued and brought home to safety. She had often pondered for years what she would do if, by absurd chance, she encountered those hideous faces she recognized as her abductors. She had thought of

23

how she'd torture them; tie them up from a ceiling by their nose hairs while continually jabbing their midsections with a hot poker. All sorts of depraved thoughts entered her mind which almost obscured her ability to live a normal life. She eventually sought hypnosis as a means by which to repress these unsettling, negative desires. And then, one day, she encountered one of them while on holiday; the ringleader of all the humiliation she was forced to endure those many years ago. There he was…staring her right in the face, but not being able to place her. But, oh, she placed *him*, and placed him **bloody well!!!**

ANNABELL: *(Slight pause, timidly.)* She…killed him?

CYNTHIA: No. She invited him over for tea. *(She sips, intensely.)*

ANNABELL: *(Slight pause.)* Oh. Really?

CYNTHIA: Yes.

ANNABELL: *(Slight pause.)* Hm. Sort of what…you've done with me, yes?

CYNTHIA: Yes.

ANNABELL: As a sort of…zen-like catharsis, if you will.

CYNTHIA: Yes.

ANNABELL: Quite admirable, I must say.

CYNTHIA: Why is that?

ANNABELL: Well, I mean, considering…

CYNTHIA: Considering what?

ANNABELL: Considering that you've…witnessed a devastating occurrence, one that would encourage, at the very least, a volatile display from the average spouse, and yet you've so eloquently risen above it,…by and large. I've conveyed my remorse and you've accepted it. And you've been gracious

24

enough to have me into your home for tea, as if nothing had happened. Yes, you've said some pointed things to me today, but I bloody deserved it. Why, I'm almost moved to tears at your restraint. I can't say that I would do the same if I caught *my* husband with another woman. And yet, despite all you must be going through, you've...you've proven yourself to be a truly centered individual, Cynthia. You know that carnal indulgence is merely fleeting and that our relationships with those close to us are, ultimately, so much more gratifying. *(Slight pause, near tears.)* Even though we only just met that fateful day, 2 weeks ago, when you discovered your husband and I completely and sweatily unclad in your bed,...I must say, Cynthia, that...I'd be crippled if I lost your friendship.

CYNTHIA: *(Slight pause, absorbing, with similar emotion.)* That's very sweet. Very kind, Annabell. And I apologize for my pointed words.

ANNABELL: Oh, no.

CYNTHIA: Yes.

ANNABELL: No.

CYNTHIA: Well, let's agree to disagree, then.

ANNABELL: Agreed.

(They share a chuckle, as if all is forgotten.)

CYNTHIA: More tea?!

ANNABELL: I'd love some.

(CYNTHIA pours tea for ANNABELL. They both resume their original positions, gazing out and embracing their tea. A moment.)

I hope it won't be awkward when Robert comes home.

CYNTHIA: Oh, Robert won't be coming home.

ANNABELL: *(Slight pause.)* You're not divorcing, are you?!

CYNTHIA: Oh heavens no!

ANNABELL: Oh, I'm so glad to hear it.

CYNTHIA: Not at all.

ANNABELL: Out of town on business, is he?

CYNTHIA: No, actually, he's in the morgue.

ANNABELL: *(Nearly choking on her tea...)* You've bloody killed him?!!!

CYNTHIA: *(Guffaws...)* Oh, God, no! It was a heart attack. Last Tuesday, I believe.

ANNABELL: Robert had a fatal heart attack last Tuesday?

CYNTHIA: Yes. *(She sips.)*

ANNABELL: *(Slight pause.)* Well,...you're handling it very well.

CYNTHIA: Why shouldn't I?

ANNABELL: Well,...considering.

CYNTHIA: Considering what?

ANNABELL: Considering the fact that...he was your husband.

CYNTHIA: *(Slight pause, realizing.)* Yes, I suppose that's true. *(Slight pause.)* Well, how are *you* holding up?

ANNABELL: Well, I...I suppose I shouldn't be grieving more than *you*, yes? It *was* only a sexual foray, as you said.

CYNTHIA: One would certainly *think* I'd be the more devastated.

ANNABELL: Well,...yes.

CYNTHIA: Hm.

(*CYNTHIA looks out pensively, as does, eventually, ANNABELL.*)

ANNABELL: Then again,…he *was* cheating on you.

CYNTHIA: Yes, and then there's that.

ANNABELL: Yet you had been together for 12 years

CYNTHIA: And then there's that.

ANNABELL: And yet, who knows how many affairs he had in that time.

CYNTHIA: (*Slight pause, subtly annoyed.*) Well,…I'd prefer to think you were the only one.

ANNABELL: (*Slight pause, almost flattered.*) Really?

CYNTHIA: (*Slight pause, resentfully,…then regretfully.*) Well, I didn't say I was ecstatic about it. Anyway, if there *was* one, who's to say there weren't others.

(*As they both look out, pondering this bitterly …for a moment…*)

ANNABELL/CYNTHIA: Bastard.

(*A still, embittered moment, before…*)

CYNTHIA: (*Brightly.*) More tea?

ANNABELL: Yes, please.

(*CYNTHIA pours, before they both face out; smiling obliviously and embracing their tea.*)

(*Lights Out.*)

DANIEL DAMIANO

End of Play

SPELL

SPELL

Spell received its World Premiere as part of
Algonquin Theatre's 1st Annual One-Act Festival,
July 2008, in New York City,
with the following cast and director:

ALBERT.....................Michael Janove
ELSA...........................Kathryn Kates

Directed by the Author

Artistic Director: Tony Sportiello

Spell was subsequently revived as part of *The World is My Cheesecake*, an Evening of One-Act Plays by Daniel Damiano, produced by Mind The Gap Theatre Company and fandango 4 productions, September 2011, in New York City, with Michael Janove as Albert and Sue Glausen as Elsa. Directed by the Author

Cast of Characters

ALBERT - 70's. Husband of Elsa. Initially cantankerous.

ELSA – 70's. Wife of Albert. Seemingly less aware, at first.

Somewhere. Afternoon. The present.

ALBERT & ELSA sit in wheelchairs, facing out. A moment.

ALBERT: Saw the doctor t'day.

ELSA: Which one?

ALBERT: *(Slight pause. Begrudgingly.)* Dr. Whitcomb.

ELSA: Whit*who*?

ALBERT: Whitcomb.

ELSA: Whitson…?

ALBERT: *COMB.* Like what I'd use if I could still groom myself.

ELSA: Dr. Comb?

ALBERT: WHITcomb. WHIT – COMB. For Godsakes, he's your doctor too.

ELSA: What's he; ear, nose and throat?

ALBERT: He's our primary doctor.

ELSA: I thought that was Ullheimer.

ALBERT: Who?!

ELSA: Ullheimer!

ALBERT: You don't have Alzheimer's, Elsa. Jus' short term memory.

ELSA: No, our primary doctor is ULLheimer.

ALBERT: **Whitcomb** is our primary doctor. I don't know who the hell "Ullheimer" is.

ELSA: Whitcomb?

ALBERT: Yes, f'Godsakes.

ELSA: Maybe Ullheimer's our gynecologist.

ALBERT: **Our** gynecologist?

ELSA: What?

ALBERT: I said… Forget it. Anyway, I went t'see Whitcomb t'day.

ELSA: Who's he?

ALBERT: Our primary doctor.

ELSA: I can't hear ya'.

ALBERT: OUR PRIMARY DOCTOR!

ELSA: Oh, yeah. What did he say?

ALBERT: He said I'm in bad shape.

ELSA: What's wrong?

ALBERT: Anything'n everything. I got somethin' called fibracolloidalcel…cel…cel…

ELSA: What the…?

ALBERT: Hold on. I'm still tryin' t'say it. Fibracolloidalcel…cel…cel… Ah, f'get it.

ELSA: What the hell is that?

ALBERT: It's what I got. How the hell do *I* know what it is. I'm not a doctor. I can't even pronounce it. All I know is I got fibracolloidalcel…cel…cel…

ELSA: But…

ALBERT: Hold on, I think I'm close. Fibracolloidalcel…cel…cel… Ah, f'get it. However the hell y'say it, I got it. n'it ain't good.

(A moment, as they gaze out.)

ELSA: What'd he recommend?

ALBERT: Waiting.

ELSA: Waiting?

ALBERT: Yep.

ELSA: Waiting for what?

ALBERT: Waiting for death.

ELSA: *(Taken aback.)* Oh. *(Slight pause, timidly.)* How long?

ALBERT: As long as I can stand it.

ELSA: Stand what?

ALBERT: As long as I can stand the illness.

ELSA: What illness?

ALBERT: I jus' told you. I've been diagnosed with Fibracol-loidalcel...cel...cel... Ah, Jesus Christmas. Forget it. I have an incurable, *unpronounceable* disease, alright?!!!

ELSA: What are the symptoms?

ALBERT: What the hell does *that* matter? I'm dying.

ELSA: I understand, Albert, but I'm asking. I can ask what the symptoms of your illness are.

ALBERT: Loss of life.

ELSA: Loss of what?

ALBERT: LIFE!

ELSA: He didn't tell you anything more specific?

ALBERT: Whata' y'need specifics for? *"You're dying"* is all y'need t'hear.

ELSA: Albert, my God, you should get a second opinion.

ALBERT: Who needs a second opinion when the first is from a doctor we've been seein' for years.

ELSA: Who cares if we've been seein' him for years. He could be wrong.

ALBERT: He's not wrong!

ELSA: Albert, you're being ridiculous.

ALBERT: Look, I have fibracolloidalcel...cel...cel...

ELSA: Stop that. You're gonna' hurt yourself.

ALBERT: What the hell does it matter?

ELSA: It matters to *me*. I don't wana' see you drivin' yourself crazy. Now just relax. Regardless a' what whoever told you, you're not dead yet. So just enjoy the day.

ALBERT: Enjoy the day. You might as well hand me a plate full a' nails and say *"Enjoy your meal."*

ELSA: Albert!

ALBERT: What?!

ELSA: *(Slight pause.)* I forgot what I was gonna' say.

ALBERT: It's just as well. There's nothing *to* say. Let's just be silent. That's all I wana' hear is my own breathing, which I won't doing be doing for long, anyway.

(A moment, as they both look out...)

ELSA: If you *are* dying, the children should be here.

ALBERT: Whose children?

ELSA: Ours. Who else's?

ALBERT: Elsa, we don't have children.

ELSA: *(Slight pause.)* We don't?

ALBERT: No.

ELSA: I coulda' sworn…

ALBERT: We don't.

(*A moment.*)

ELSA: Well, where's the cat?

ALBERT: The what?

ELSA: Our cat. The cat should at least be here.

ALBERT: Elsa, we don't have a cat.

ELSA: No, I'm sure we have a cat.

ALBERT: We don't have a Goddamn cat, Elsa. We *had* one.

ELSA: We *had* one?

ALBERT: Over 10 years ago.

ELSA: What happened?

ALBERT: He died.

ELSA: He died?

ALBERT: Well, what do y'*think* woulda' happened? You think he's in the Witness Protection Program? Cats don't live as long as we do. My God, he musta' been 24 when he died.

ELSA: That's terrible.

ALBERT: Yeah, well…

ELSA: *(Slight pause, digesting.)* How did he die?

ALBERT: He was old, that's how he died. F'Godsakes, I jus' tell you *I'm* dying and you're asking how the cat died over a decade ago.

ELSA: Who said you're dying?

ALBERT: Dr. Whitcomb.

ELSA: Who?

ALBERT: WHITCOMB! I told you, he said I have fibracolloi-dalcel...cel...cel...

ELSA: *(Suddenly, as if on reflex.)* Fibracolloidalcelemisitosis?

ALBERT: *(Stunned.)* That's it. How d'*you* know how t'say it?

ELSA: *(Surprised herself.)* I don't know. It jus' came t'me, I suppose.

ALBERT: *(Then, sadly...)* Well, in any case,...that't it.

(A moment, they both look out, lugubriously.)

ELSA: *(Suddenly optimistic.)* I read somewhere that if you can spell your disease, you can cure yourself of it.

ALBERT: Where the hell did ya' read *that*?

ELSA: Off the back of a Shredded Wheat box.

ALBERT: *(As if typical.)* A Shredded Wheat box. Nice.

ELSA: I think it's an ancient Hindu belief.

ALBERT: Since when are we Hindu?

ELSA: I don't think you have to be Hindu to believe a Hindu belief.

ALBERT: Sounds like some crazy old myth that probably never worked for the Hindus, let alone anyone else.

ELSA: You don't know that.

ALBERT: Oh, please, Elsa. I know as well as I've known about any other urban legend you've thrown up. Rhubarb cures migraines. Mint jelly keeps away mosquitoes. *That* was a good one.

ELSA: When did I say that?

ALBERT: Like five years ago. **In August,** you had me sitting in the backyard covered with it. I felt like a damn lamb chop. Took me 2 weeks to get the smell outa' my skin, and I *still* got bit t'high heaven.

ELSA: Well, I don't remember, but I'm sure I got that from a reliable source.

ALBERT: Reliable source. You probably misread the jar, f'Godsakes. And now it's the Shredded Wheat and the Hindus. Please, Elsa. I'll take a fatal diagnosis from a licensed doctor any day over an old wives' tale from a buncha' bald hippies.

ELSA: That's a terrible way to think, Albert.

ALBERT: It's knowledge, Elsa. It's fact over fiction.

ELSA: You're gonna' invest all your trust in a terminal diagnosis when you can be hopeful?

ALBERT: *(Sharply!)* Fine. Spell Neurogastreotomatisis.

ELSA: *(Slight pause, tentatively.)* Why…why on earth would I wana' spell *that…? (Slowly realizing, …)* No.

ALBERT: *(Slight pause.)* I knew you'd forget. That's why I didn't wana' bring it up.

ELSA: No.

ALBERT: Yes. Ask Dr. Whitcomb…

ELSA: Who?

ALBERT: *(With calm indulgence, this time.)* Whit-comb.

ELSA: *(Slight pause, becoming slightly frightened.)* He said I have…

ALBERT: Neurogastreotomatisis.

ELSA: *(Timidly.)* What…what is it?

ALBERT: *(Regretfully.)* I dunno'. It's some sorta'…fatal, debilitating illness.

ELSA: I…I didn't know this.

ALBERT: He jus' told ya' yesterday. You jus' forgot.

ELSA: *(Slight pause, tenuously…)* Neur…. Neuro… Neur… Neuro …

ALBERT: Neurogastreotomatisis.

ELSA: Neur…neuro…neur….neuro…

ALBERT: Neurogastreotomatisis.

ELSA: *(Slight pause, then curiously.)* How come you can say my illness but you can't pronounce your own?

ALBERT: *(Thinks.)* I…I dunno'. *(Slight pause.)* Fibracolloidalcel…cel…cel… Ah, damn it t'hell!!!

ELSA: *(A sudden shooting pain…)* Oh, dear…!

ALBERT: What?!

ELSA: I feel…I feel terrible, my stomach…I feel like…

ALBERT: Dear God, are you dying?

ELSA: What're you asking <u>Him</u> for? I'm the one writhing in paiiiiiiiiii....!!!

ALBERT: ELSA?!!!

ELSA: I'm...I can't swallow... I feel like I'm...like I'm burning... Albert,...!

ALBERT: Yes?!

ELSA: Get me my medication.

ALBERT: What medication?

ELSA: Didn't the doctor prescribe medication?

ALBERT: He didn't prescribe anything.

ELSA: What?!

ALBERT: He said there's nothing that can be done.

ELSA: What about painkillers?!

ALBERT; He said you shouldn't experience any pain. Just a gradual unconsciousness.

ELSA: *(Another shooting pain...)* OWWW!!!

ALBERT: Elsa,...?!!!

ELSA: I think I'm...I'm...

ALBERT: I'll call Dr. Whitcomb.

ELSA: Who?!

ALBERT: *(Looking out...)* DR. WHITCOMB! DR. WHIT-COMB, HELP! **MY WIFE IS IN PAIN!!!**

ELSA: What can *he* do, Albert?! Isn't he just waiting for us to die?!

ALBERT: *(An anxious beat.)* Well,...yes, but...

ELSA: Then what the hell do we need *him* for?!!!

ALBERT: But...Elsa, we have t'do *something*. I...I can't just let you...

ELSA: *(Another shooting pain...)* Oh, dear...!

ALBERT: Elsa...

ELSA: Owwwww, it hurts....!

ALBERT: ELSAAAAAAAAAAA,...!!!!

ELSA: *(Suddenly and desperately.)* NEUROGASTREOTOM-ATISIS!!!!

ALBERT: What the hell...?!!!

ELSA: *(Straining and writhing in pain.)* Neurogastreotoma-tisis!!! N – E – U – R....O – G...A....S...

ALBERT: Elsa, what on earth... ?!

ELSA : SSSSSSSH! T- R - E-O- T- O -M – A....

ALBERT : Elsa,...!

ELSA: T – I – S-.......I................. *(As if in labor, a last push...)* **EEEEHHHHHSSSSSS!!!**

> *(A moment, as ELSA...gradually comes out of her contortion and slowly sits upright, while touching her stomach. She smiles elatedly...)*

> *(A moment.)*

ALBERT: El...Elsa?

ELSA: Albert,...I'm....I'm healed.

ALBERT: Your...?

ELSA: The pain is gone. I'm healed, Albert.

ALBERT: You're…you're not…you're not dying?

ELSA: No.

ALBERT: Are you sure?

> *(A distinct moment, before ELSA rises, swiftly and elegantly, as if she is about to dance.)*

ALBERT: It's…it's some sorta' miracle or…

ELSA: It musta' been the spelling.

ALBERT: The what?

ELSA: It was the spelling, Albert. What I read on the Shredded Wheat box. Look at me!

ALBERT: No, it…it has t'be a strange freak of nature, a coincidence…

ELSA: Albert, are you crazy? You think it's a coincidence that my symptoms just went away?

ALBERT: Well,…

ELSA: **Albert, look at me.**

> *(ELSA looks at ALBERT deeply for a moment, before holding out her hands for him. He slowly takes them but, to his regret, cannot rise.)*

ALBERT: I…I can't.

ELSA: I want you to stand with me, Albert.

ALBERT: I can't stand, Elsa. I'm not well. If I try, I'm liable to tip over like a condemned building.

ELSA: Albert, …

ALBERT: *(A sudden panic…)* **I can't!!!** F'Godsakes, I'm a mess. My sight's going, my memory's gettin' shorter, I can't hear well, I got hot flashes, cold spells, nausea, dehydration... If I wasn't constipated, I'd probably have dysentery...

ELSA: *(Adamantly.)* Spell, Albert!

ALBERT: *(Slight pause, feebly.)* Spell...?

ELSA: Fibracolloidalcelemisitosis.

ALBERT: *(Slight pause, timidly.)* That's...that's what I have?

ELSA: Yes. Now spell it before it's too late, Albert. Say it first.

ALBERT: *(Slight pause.)* Fi...fi...

ELSA: Fibracolloidalcelemisitosis.

ALBERT: Fi...fi...

ELSA: Fibra...

ALBERT: Fi...

ELSA: Fibra...

ALBERT: Ah, the hell with it, Elsa. It'll be easier t'die.

ELSA: Albert, don't talk like that!

ALBERT: I can't even *say* it, let alone *spell* the damn thing. It's like spelling the alphabet backwards with a gun t'your head.

ELSA: Albert, you have to try, do you understand me? You have to find it within yourself. I don't wana' waste my good health on being without you!

(ALBERT looks at ELSA affectionately...before subtly sinking into his seat, his eyes becoming heavier...)

Albert?!

ALBERT: *(Becomes gradually weak...)* I feel...I feel weak, Elsa...

ELSA: *(Urgently.)* Albert, just spell it...

ALBERT: It's...it's too many letters, Elsa. I'll never...

ELSA: Albert, try. Try!

ALBERT: I...I can't...

ELSA: Albert...

ALBERT: I'm not Hindu....!

ELSA: NEITHER AM I!!! NOW SPELL THAT GODDAMN FUCKING DISEASE!!!

ALBERT: *(With great difficulty, through his weakness...)* F-I...B...R-A.....C-O-L....L....O...I...D....A...L...C...E...L...

ELSA: That's it, Albert...

ALBERT: *(His breathing is now heavier...)* E....M....I....S..I...T....O....S…….....……I……

(His eyes are half closed, his breathing labored...)

ELSA: Albert? *(Touches his hand eagerly...)* Albert, say "S". One letter left. "S"! **ALBERT?!!!** *(Utterly desperate, but softly...)* Albert?

(A moment, as ELSA, on her knees, looks up at ALBERT, who is still breathing. She is emotional but hopeful,...as she waits, with his hand in hers...as the lights fade.)

End of Play

THE DESSERT CART

THE DESSERT CART

The Dessert Cart received its World Premiere as part of Gallery Players' 7th Annual Black Box Festival, 2004, in Brooklyn, NY, with the following cast and directors:

HUSBAND...............................David Keller
WIFE...Donna Robinson
WAITER.....................................Shawn Reese
MAITRE D'/PASTRY CHEF.............Craig Colfelt

Directed by Joseph Rosswog and Ria Cooper

Artistic Director:
Heather Siobhan Curran

The Dessert Cart was subsequently revived as part of *The World is My Cheesecake*, an Evening of One-Act plays by Daniel Damiano, produced by Mind The Gap Theatre Company and fandango 4 productions, September 2011, in New York City, featuring Stuart Williams as Husband, Emma Gordon as Wife, Simon Pearl as Waiter and Justin Herfel as Maitre D'/Pastry Chef. Directed by Paula D'Alessandris

*The Dessert Cart was the recipient of the 2024 David A. Einhorn Memorial Playwriting Prize, presented by Untitled Theater Company No. 61 in NYC.

Cast of Characters

WAITER – *30s. Sharp, efficient.*

HUSBAND – *30s-40s. Well-spoken, refined.*

WIFE – *30s-40s. Well-spoken, refined.*

PASTRY CHEF – *40s. Corpulent, pleasant.*

MAITRE D' – *40s. Exudes authority, though restrained and tactful.*

The play takes place at a fine restaurant, somewhere.

The Time is the Present.

Note: The actor playing PASTRY CHEF may also double as the MAITRE D', as long as there is a clear delineation between characters in both performance and wardrobe.

The lights come up to reveal HUSBAND & WIFE across from one another at dining table, with WAITER standing between. HUSBAND and WIFE look at each other with identical grins of satisfaction. All are frozen, before...

WAITER: Was everything to your liking?

HUSBAND: Oh, most certainly.

WIFE: Absolutely.

HUSBAND & WIFE: Just wonderful!

WIFE: The veal was from the heavens.

HUSBAND: The chicken, from a much more sinful place.

> *(They ALL laugh uproariously in sync, then abruptly stop, though smiles remain.)*

WAITER: Very well. Would you desire to see...?

WIFE: Oh, yes!

HUSBAND: Most definitely!

WIFE: And two coffees, please.

HUSBAND: Yes, thank you.

WAITER: Very well. Our Master Pastry Chef will present the dessert cart.

HUSBAND & WIFE: Splendid!

> *(WAITER goes off, while HUSBAND and WIFE look at one another with enhanced anticipation...)*

HUSBAND: The moment of truth.

WIFE: Oh, yes.

HUSBAND & WIFE: Indeed!

THE DESSERT CART

(The PASTRY CHEF immediately comes out with dessert cart. Atop it is the famed Marble Cheesecake, with two extremely small white cards on either side, as if merely décor.)

HUSBAND & WIFE: The famous Marble Cheesecake!

PASTRY CHEF: Yes, it is rather well regarded.

WIFE: Will you just look at that.

HUSBAND: As if observing a landmark.

WIFE: Yes.

HUSBAND: Just lovely.

WIFE: Like the Coliseum.

PASTRY CHEF: That may be a bit of an overstatement.

HUSBAND: Only to an architect.

WIFE: We'll each have a slice please.

HUSBAND: Yes, thank you.

PASTRY CHEF: Well, now sir, madam, there is also something special that you may wish to consider.

HUSBAND: More special than the famed Marble Cheesecake?!

PASTRY CHEF: Yes, I'd like to think so.

WIFE: *(Politely incredulous.)* Well, I'm afraid…

HUSBAND: …the Marble Cheesecake is the main reason we came this evening.

WIFE: That's true.

PASTRY CHEF: *(Politely amused.)* Is it now.

WIFE: Well, of course.

HUSBAND: It's world renowned.

WIFE: Not that the dinner wasn't exquisite.

HUSBAND: Oh, certainly not.

WIFE: I mean, the veal was…

HUSBAND: …and the chicken…

HUSBAND & WIFE: Just delectable!

WIFE: But that aside,…

HUSBAND: …the Marble Cheesecake was the catalyst to our patronage.

PASTRY CHEF: *(Taken somewhat aback, before…)* Well, again, I'll be more than happy to oblige if that is truly what you desire…

HUSBAND & WIFE: *(Excitedly.)* Oh, it is!

PASTRY CHEF: However, I must stress that there is a most appealing alternative that I've yet to reveal to you.

> *(HUSBAND & WIFE look at each other, politely offguarded by the CHEF's subtle persistence. The CHEF, sensing that he has made some headway…)*

Although, it is up to you, of course.

HUSBAND: *(Slight pause.)* Well, alright. We'll…we'll certainly consider it.

WIFE: Far be it for us not to ponder something prepared by such a distinguished auteur of the culinary arts.

HUSBAND: Absolutely. Please.

PASTRY CHEF: Very good.

(The CHEF, most pleased, waves his hand over cart...as HUSBAND and WIFE observe in search of another dessert, yet find nothing.)

HUSBAND: I suppose you'll tell us?

PASTRY CHEF: Oh, no. It's on the cart.

(A moment, before the PASTRY CHEF playfully lifts up cards, then places them back down on cart.)

HUSBAND & WIFE: Ah, the cards!

PASTRY CHEF: Correct.

HUSBAND: Are we to take them?

PASTRY CHEF: You may if you wish.

(HUSBAND and WIFE take their cards and read, somewhat taken aback by the content...)

HUSBAND: Oh,...well.

WIFE: Yes,...well.

HUSBAND: Certainly,...

WIFE: ...not what I expected.

HUSBAND: Not at all.

WIFE: *(To CHEF, a weak snicker.)* I thought that these were dessert menus of some kind.

HUSBAND: Yes, as did I.

PASTRY CHEF: *(Beaming.)* Oh, not an unusual assumption, I assure you.

HUSBAND: *(Delicately.)* You...composed this yourself?

PASTRY CHEF: Oh, yes.

WIFE: *(Masking pity...)* Very...

HUSBAND: ...profound.

WIFE: Yes.

HUSBAND: Yes.

HUSBAND & WIFE: *(Awkwardly appeasing.)* In...deed.

PASTRY CHEF: *(With great satisfaction.)* My pleasure.

> *(The PASTRY CHEF exits off with dessert cart, much to the awkward surprise of HUSBAND & WIFE. WAITER immediately comes on with bill.)*

WAITER: Sir.

> *(...as WAITER places bill upon table.)*

HUSBAND: *(Slight pause.)* What is this?

WAITER: It's your bill, sir. Take your time, please.

> *(HUSBAND looks at WIFE, then...)*

HUSBAND: *(to WAITER.)* I'm sorry, but isn't it customary in a fine restaurant to present the bill *after* we've had our final course?

WAITER: I'm sorry, sir. I was under the impression that you had.

WIFE: Well, we haven't.

WAITER: No?

HUSBAND: No, we haven't. We'd assumed that the Master Pastry Chef was bringing out the special.

WAITER: The special what, sir?

HUSBAND: The special dessert, of course.

WAITER: No, he isn't sir.

WIFE: He isn't?

WAITER: No, madam.

> *(HUSBAND and WIFE look at each other, baffled, before…*

HUSBAND: *(Goodnaturedly.)* Well, in any case, we did want the cheesecake in the first place. So whenever you're ready.

WAITER: Ready for what, sir?

HUSBAND: To bring us our dessert.

WIFE: And two coffees, please.

HUSBAND: Yes, thank you.

> *(HUSBAND & WIFE look at each other with grins of anticipation, as before…before…)*

WAITER: *(Slight pause.)* I'm sorry. Are you…serious?

HUSBAND: *(Slight pause.)* Of course. Why wouldn't we be?

WIFE: We never make light of something that we've so anticipated.

> *(WAITER remains subtly perplexed.)*

HUSBAND: Is there something wrong?

WAITER: *(Then, snobbishly…)* We have a bit of an appetite, I see.

HUSBAND: I'm sorry?

WAITER: *(Curtly.)* A moment, please.

> *(WAITER signals for MAITRE D', as HUSBAND and WIFE look at each other oddly.)*

(MAITRE D' enters. WAITER whispers to him as HUS-BAND and WIFE awkwardly observe...before...)

MAITRE D': I see. *(To HUSBAND & WIFE.)* Good evening, madam. Sir.

HUSBAND & WIFE: Good evening.

MAITRE D': *(Most pleasantly.)* Your waiter has just informed me.

HUSBAND: Of what?

MAITRE D': Of the dilemma.

WIFE: Is there one?

MAITRE D': With regards to your final course.

HUSBAND: What about it?

MAITRE D': You've already received it.

WIFE: No, we haven't.

MAITRE D': Oh, I believe you certainly have, madam.

HUSBAND: I'm not sure if I understand the confusion. I mean, it should be fairly obvious that we haven't received anything. There's no plates...

WIFE: No coffee.

MAITRE D': I'm referring to the Wisdom.

HUSBAND & WIFE: The what?

MAITRE D': The Wisdom.

HUSBAND: *(Slight pause.)* I'm sorry but I'm afraid you've lost us.

WIFE: Was that the special that the Pastry Chef was going to show us?

MAITRE D': I'm referring to the cards.

HUSBAND: What about them?

MAITRE D': You've read them, correct?

HUSBAND: Yes.

MAITRE D': *(An enlarged smile.)* Yes, as I assumed.

WIFE: *(Slight pause.)* What does that have to do with anything?

MAITRE D': *(Tactfully.)* Well, with all due respect, all patrons who frequent this establishment settle on one option or the other. To select both is simply…a display of gluttony.

HUSBAND & WIFE: Gluttony?!

MAITRE D' & WAITER: Yes.

HUSBAND: *(Slight pause.)* Wait a mome… Are you saying that the content of these little cards is actually considered a course in itself?

MAITRE D': *(Smiling.)* Well, of course, sir.

WIFE: *Wisdom.*

MAITRE D' & WAITER: Indeed.

MAITRE D': We'd assumed that that was understood.

WIFE: Well, no, it certainly wasn't.

HUSBAND: Certainly not.

MAITRE D': Well, then on behalf of our staff, I wish to apologize for any misunderstanding. I sincerely hope that this won't serve to mar your experience.

(HUSBAND & WIFE look at each other, before breaking into a relieved chuckle...)

WIFE: Au contrar.

HUSBAND: By no means, gentlemen.

MAITRE D': Wonderful.

WIFE: I must say, we've always had an appreciation for the more unusual presentations.

HUSBAND: Though I'm afraid this one does take the cake.

(ALL Laugh uproariously at the horrid pun, then abruptly stop...before...)

WIFE: And so...we will take ours.

MAITRE D': Madam?

WIFE: The Marble Cheesecake.

HUSBAND: And two coffees, please.

WIFE: Yes, thank you.

(MAITRE D' and WAITER look at each other in disbelief, as HUSBAND & WIFE anticipate...)

MAITRE D': I'm sorry, sir, madam, but...there appears to some confusion.

HUSBAND: Regarding what?

MAITRE D': Well, you see, you've already had your final course.

WIFE: *(Slight pause.)* Excuse me?

MAITRE D': Yes.

HUSBAND: I'm sorry, but I thought we had just resolved this misunderstanding.

WIFE: As did I.

MAITRE D': Yes, as did I, but…perhaps there needs to be some clarification.

HUSBAND: As to what?

MAITRE D': You see, you have already been privy to the Wisdom. Therefore, consuming an actual dessert will only serve to negate your original selection.

WIFE: I beg your pardon.

HUSBAND: We did not "select" Wisdom.

WIFE: Certainly not.

MAITRE D': *(Pleasantly.)* Nonetheless, it is now within you both.

HUSBAND: Well, through no intent of our own, I assure you.

WIFE: If anything, it was rather cunningly presented to us.

MAITRE D' & WAITER: Cunningly!

HUSBAND: It most certainly was.

WIFE: Most certainly.

HUSBAND: We only inquired under the assumption that the "alternative" was another dessert.

WIFE: Yes.

HUSBAND: Actual food.

WIFE: Yes.

HUSBAND: Cake, pie, gelato!

HUSBAND & WIFE: Something digestable!

MAITRE D': *(Defensive.)* Did you not agree that it was "profound"?

WIFE: What?!

HUSBAND: My God, we were appeasing the man.

WIFE: Who knew how he would react if we responded truthfully to his utterly banal contrivance?

HUSBAND: We've heard of the madness to which chef's succumb, not unlike abstract painters or computer programmers.

MAITRE D': I can assure you that our Master Pastry Chef is by no means mad, sir!

WIFE: No, he just wears a chef's hat and fancies himself as Confucius.

MAITRE D': You are aware that true sustenance is a state of mind.

(HUSBAND & WIFE rise in sync...)

HUSBAND & WIFE: How dare you?!!!

WIFE: We are far from ignorant with regards to philosophical nature, and it is not the place of a restaurant staff to question that!

HUSBAND: What one desires is what they desire because they have a right to desire it, and that is all you need to concern yourself with!

MAITRE D': And you "desire" marble cheesecake.

HUSBAND & WIFE: YES!!!

MAITRE D': Therefore, obliterating your initial selection.

HUSBAND: For the last time, sir, it was not our "selection",...

WIFE: It was coercion!

HUSBAND: Exactly!

WAITER: *Cunning.*

HUSBAND & WIFE: Indeed!

> *(A moment, before HUSBAND and WIFE sit down in sync.)*

> *(A moment, before…)*

HUSBAND: Well?

MAITRE D' & WAITER: "Well" what, sir?

WIFE: May we have our dessert, please?

> *(MAITRE D' and WAITER look at each other, before…)*

MAITRE D': *(Begrudgingly pleasant.)* Of course, madam. Sir.

> *(MAITRE D' indicates to WAITER, who in turn removes bill from table and goes off, immediately coming back with two slices of marble cheesecake, which he places before HUSBAND and WIFE.)*

WIFE: And two coffees, please.

HUSBAND: Yes, thank you.

WAITER: Of course.

> *(MAITRE D' observes with vivid contempt as HUSBAND & WIFE, oblivious, gawk at their plates before them with great satisfaction…before WAITER immediately comes back out with coffees. HUSBAND and WIFE then, in sync, make their first indentation into the cake…before…)*

HUSBAND & WIFE: *(Sensing, they look out. A beat, then…)*
Hm.

HUSBAND: If I didn't know better, I'd think…

WIFE: …everybody's staring at us.

HUSBAND: Yes.

WIFE: Why do you suppose?

HUSBAND: It's not as if they…

WIFE: No.

MAITRE D' & WAITER: *(Haughtily.)* Yes.

HUSBAND: These people aren't having the marble cheesecake for dessert?

WIFE: None of them?

MAITRE D' & WAITER; No.

HUSBAND: *(Slight pause, observing plate.)* But…but this is the only dessert they serve here.

WIFE: *(Observing plate...)* It's been hailed in all of the most respected dining periodicals.

HUSBAND: Why would they all not have it?

MAITRE D': Because it is not the only option.

WIFE: *(Weakly incredulous.)* But someone's had it at *some* point. I mean, this…this is a famous cake.

HUSBAND: Yes.

WIFE: How could word get out about its sheer decadence if no one has ever…?

(HUSBAND and WIFE come to a realization…!)

HUSBAND: Because…

HUSBAND & WIFE: …critics have!

MAITRE D' & WAITER: Yes.

MAITRE D': After all, they are paid to try it.

WAITER: However,…no one else is.

MAITRE D': Therefore, …no one else has to.

WIFE: *(Weakly...)* But…

HUSBAND: *(Weakly...)* …we want to.

MAITRE D': Then by all means.

WIFE: *(Slight pause.)* We…we can?

MAITRE D'; Most certainly. It is your "right", correct?

(An odd moment, as HUSBAND and WIFE look at each other warily…before…)

HUSBAND: *(With hesitancy...)* Well, then let's…

(They motion to cake with identical ambivalence…before WIFE drops fork onto plate, as if a gasp. HUSBAND notices this but continues on before…slamming his fork down onto table!)

HUSBAND: DAMNIT! It's not as if we're oblivious. We've…we've attended the finest universities. We've indulged in the likes of Socrates, Plato, Aristotle…

WIFE: The *I Ching*…

HUSBAND: DesCartes, Kierkegaard, Nietzche…

WIFE: *The Art of Happiness*…

HUSBAND: We're very much attuned to what…what…

WIFE: …what…what…

HUSBAND & WIFE: *(As they rise…)* We just want that God-damned cake!!!

WIFE: Without ridicule!

HUSBAND: Without judgment!

WAITER: *(Smugly.)* Neither are on the menu.

HUSBAND: *(Slight pause.)* So they can't order it then. *(Looking out, with maniacal passion.)* They can only sit with their choice, right? And we can eat and revel in their envy, correct? WE'RE HAVING THE MARBLE CHEESECAKE, DO YOU HEAR ME?!!! AND THEY CAN ONLY LIVE WITH THEIR REGRET, BECAUSE THEY DON'T HAVE THE COURAGE TO DEMAND WHAT THEY *REALLY* CAME FOR. THEY'VE CATERED TO YOUR MORBID DESIRES SO THAT THEY…THEY CAN FEEL AS IF THEY'RE PART OF SOMETHING THAT'S BEEN MISSING FROM THEIR LIVES. THEY LACK MENTAL NOURISHMENT AND ARE EASILY SATISFIED WITH SOME CONCOCTED PROVERB. TO THEM, IT'S SUBSTANTIAL. TO *US*, IT'S…IT'S MERELY… *(Guffaws mockingly, then…)*

> *(HUSBAND hurriedly sits, voraciously picks up plate, holds fork, looks at WIFE, who now appears torn and ill at ease at his display…)*

Well?

WIFE: *(Stalling.)* What?

HUSBAND: Aren't you…?

WIFE: *(Slight pause.)* I'm…I'm not sure now.

HUSBAND: My dear, this is our right. We're patrons. They have to cater to us, not us to them. You can't succumb to…

WIFE: I'm not! I'm just…thinking.

HUSBAND: About what?

WIFE: I'm just...not certain now. Let me just...

HUSBAND: But...

MAITRE D': Sir, perhaps...

HUSBAND: I AM HAVING A DISCUSSION WITH MY WIFE, DO YOU MIND?!

MAITRE D': Very well, sir.

HUSBAND: *(Slight pause, breathes...)* My dear...

> *(WIFE abruptly yet committedly sits, then gently pushes her plate away.)*

> *(A moment.)*

WIFE: It just dawned on me, ...seeing you there.

HUSBAND: Seeing me where?

WIFE: Maybe...maybe...

HUSBAND: What?!

WIFE: *(Slight pause, then with difficulty.)* Maybe...we aren't as enlightened as we've always assumed. Maybe for all our erudition, we still...we still place more value in... This cake will only be before us for a short while before it's eventually devoured. Then it will become what everything else becomes; A desire of the moment, then a memory... And how long will it last? How long should it...when it doesn't matter? We can always say we were...someplace, ate somewhere, had something exquisite...only to be alone, across a table, at another restaurant, saying nothing to each other except with regards to the menu. Hoping that our meal is respectable...in lieu of... *(Slight pause, finally and sadly.)* I'm not satisfied.

> *(WIFE turns out, unable to face HUSBAND...)*

HUSBAND: *(Pierced.)* But…we've had such nice…meals.

WIFE: Yes, we have.

HUSBAND: And…that doesn't…?

WIFE: No, it doesn't. Not anymore. I can't go on acting as if it does.

(An odd moment, before HUSBAND rises…)

HUSBAND: *(Suddenly and hostile, to Maitre D' & Waiter…)* I blame you for this! This is abominable what's gone on here this evening. Well-intentioned patrons, and we've been accosted by you and your feeble-minded clientele. You should be ashamed of yourselves, running such a criminal establishment! What do I owe you for this catastrophic evening?! *(Reaches in pocket angrily…)* And we're only paying for the dinner, not the so-called *"Wisdom"* because we didn't request it. And not for the famed Marble Cheesecake, because it was unlawfully withheld from us, if not by force then most certainly by intimidation which, I might add, we did NOT fall prey to. We simply couldn't BARE to digest a THING in our current states of dismay! *(Finally pulling out wallet.)* Well?!

MAITRE D': *(Calm and removed.)* Very well, sir.

(MAITRE D' motions to WAITER, who promptly goes off. MAITRE D' follows.)

HUSBAND: I didn't suppose there'd be an "alternative" to the bill!

(HUSBAND then hesitantly sits, observes pensive WIFE awkwardly.)

(A moment, before…)

Well, I'm… This has certainly turned out to be…most disturbing, hasn't it? *(Slight pause.)* Are…? Do…? *(Slight pause, grasping now…)* Your veal was…?

(A jarringly odd moment, as WIFE remains pensively still...before WAITER returns with 2 documents and a large plume pen, which he presents to HUSBAND...)

WAITER: Sir.

HUSBAND: *(Looks oddly at pen, before looking down at papers...)* What is...? Divorce papers?!!!

(MAITRE D' immediately rolls out a cart, atop which rests only a gavel, as he speaks the following...)

MAITRE D': You only need sign and your meal will be taken care of.

(HUSBAND, at first outraged, then looks defeatedly at WIFE, who looks back with regretful acceptance.)

HUSBAND: Was this your intention all along?

WIFE: Of course not. I'm as surprised as you are.

(HUSBAND looks down at paper, then slowly back up at WIFE.)

HUSBAND: Is...is this what you want?

WIFE: *(With delicate certainty.)* It is now.

(A moment, before HUSBAND reluctantly signs. WAITER then presents documents and pen to WIFE...)

WAITER: Madam?

(WIFE looks at HUSBAND, before firmly signing. WAITER then presents documents to MAITRE D' at podium.)

(To Maitre D'.)

Sir?

MAITRE D': Thank you.

(MAITRE D' signs as…)

HUSBAND: *You* have authority?

MAITRE D': Oh, yes. *(Dots signature, pleasantly.)* You are both hereby divorced!

> *(MAITRE D' then picks up gavel and SLAMS it down upon podium!)*

> *(Most kindly.)*

The best to you both.

> *(MAITRE D' immediately rolls off podium, along with papers, as WAITER removes WIFE's plate and coffee…)*

WAITER: I bid you good evening, madam. Sir, your cake will be on the house.

> *(WAITER exits off.)*

> *(After a moment, WIFE rises…)*

WIFE: *(A joyful realization, to herself…)* I didn't expect it would come to this but…I must say, I feel…wonderful! I can…I can breathe better, see more clearly… It's as if the world has become my oyster. Or better yet,…my cheesecake! *(Laughs elatedly…)* Yes, the world has become my cheesecake…and I'M holding the fork!!! *(Suddenly, she looks out, waves…)* HAVE A WONDERFUL EVENING, MY FELLOW PATRONS!!! *(Slight pause, to HUSBAND, profoundly yet delicately.)* Goodbye.

> *(A beat, before WIFE proudly exits, as HUSBAND rises…)*

> *(A moment, before HUSBAND looks out at patrons, awkwardly, then sits, dejectedly. He ponders a moment…before taking notice of WIFE's card still on table. He subtly slides his hand over to it, picks it up, reads to himself…before weakly snickering…*

HUSBAND: The same as mine.

(HUSBAND guffaws at its seeming banality...before fading into his prior despondency. He unconsciously drops card onto floor.)

(A moment, before he turns to cake. At first, he is apathetic to it,...before gradually picking up fork...and consuming a small portion. He absorbs it in his mouth...as if in gradual ecstasy...)

Mmmm, oh my...

(...before indulging once again. This time, a slightly larger portion...)

Mmmm, oh God that's good! Oh, my dear God...!

(He savors it with increased relish, before sipping his coffee...and eagerly consuming another substantial mouthful...)

Oh...my... Oh, my... this is just...this is just from the heavens! Purely, from the heavens... Oh, dear... OH, DEAR...!!!

(He laughs gleefully, before ravenously consuming another large portion with his hands...)

OH, MY GOD!!!

(He continues to gorge and laugh...as the lights fade out...)

End of Play

1

THE LEPERS

THE LEPERS

The Lepers received its World Premiere as part of Ensemble Studio Theatre's 37th Marathon of One-Act Plays, May-June 2019, in New York City, with the following cast and director:

VIN.................................Joseph Cassesse
VANESSA...................Wilma Cespedes-Rivera

Directed by Matthew Penn

Artistic Director: William Carden

Cast of Characters

VIN - 36, male.   Lanky, unfiltered, Italian-American, from Queens.

VANESSA – 29, female.   Tough but vulnerable, Puerto Rican-American, from the Bronx.

A coffee shop in the city, late in the evening.

Late January, 2017.

THE LEPERS

Vin and Vanessa at a coffee shop,
with a cup before each of them.

VIN: Then she died too. That was after my Aunt Charlene and Aunt Theresa. Same thing.

VANESSA: Same thing?

VIN: All 3 of 'em – heart attacks. My mother and her two sistas. I mean, you had to see 'em. Huuuge. They didn't care. Their whole life, eatin' everything. Processed shit, everything. If the three of 'em tried walkin' side by side on a sidewalk, one had to walk in the damn street.

VANESSA: What?!

VIN: That's how big they were.

VANESSA: Wow.

VIN: My Aunt Charlene even got stuck in a sewer once.

VANESSA: No fuckin' way.

VIN: Oh, yeah.

VANESSA: C'mon, Vin...

VIN: Believe me, I'm not that creative.

VANESSA: Jesus...

VIN: Got written up in the *Post* too.

VANESSA: No!

VIN: Oh, yeah.

VANESSA: It was actually in the news?!

VIN: Fuckin' embarrassing, man.

VANESSA: Jesus…

VIN: Yeah. But I said, hey, I ain't gonna' be like that. Whatever I do, I ain't gonna' be like them.

VANESSA: Well, you're right about that. Y'thin as a rail.

VIN; Sure, 'cause I got addicted to somethin' else, y'see? That's the irony. In the end, it's the same thing. Y'see? Whether I'm a fuckin' rhinoceros in a muumuu or a skinny guy at a bar until last call. Same thing.

VANESSA: Yeah, I see whatcha' sayin'…

VIN: Twinkies or scotch'n coke. Same thing.

VANESSA: But you're almost at 5 months now, right?

VIN: Yeah.

VANESSA: So that's different.

VIN: Whata' y'mean?

VANESSA: That's different than what you came from, right? I mean, was your moms ever able to stop eatin' Ring Dings for 5 months?

VIN: Are you kiddin'?

VANESSA: That's what I'm sayin'. So you ain't like her or your aunts n'whoever else.

VIN: Hey, I am'n I'm not.

VANESSA: I ain't sayin' it ain't tough. I don't know how you done it, man. 5 months.

VIN: Hey, I'm doin' it like any a' the rest of 'em. One day at a time...

VANESSA: *(Over "One day at a time...")* One day at a time, yeah, yeah, yeah.

VIN: Hey, lemme tell ya', when I first started goin' n'I heard that, I was like *why does everyone here talk like a T-Shirt?*

VANESSA: Exactly!

VIN: Everything sounds like a fuckin' ad campaign, right?

VANESSA: Yeah, right.

VIN; Right, but it's like an apple a day. It's a cliché but at the same time, why is it?

VANESSA: 'cause it's true.

VIN; Fuckin' A. Exactly. Don't ya' think if my mother put down the Chips Ahoy for a month and had an apple a day, she woulda' had a chance a' *not* bein' buried by a forklift?

VANESSA: *(Trying not to laugh...)* Oh, snap...!

VIN: *(Smiling...)* It's true.

VANESSA: Holy shit...

VIN: Sure, laugh.

VANESSA: Vin, I'm not, I swear...

VIN: You're bitin' on your cheek so hard, you're bleedin' outa' your mouth. Whata' y'mean you're not?!

VANESSA: *(Laughing a bit harder as a result of trying to resist...)* I'm not laughin' at her, I swear.

VIN: If that's not laughin', what is it, gargling?

VANESSA: Vin, stop...

VIN: Go ahead, laugh. It's funny. Are you kiddin'? I laughed then, why shouldn't you laugh now.

VANESSA: *(Easing out of her laughter...)* It ain't funny, though. It's sad, man.

VIN: *(Smiles at Vanessa's attempt...)* Yeah, anyway...

VANESSA: It is!

VIN: *(Smiling at her restrained laughter...)* I know it is, Queen of the Obvious. Jesus... *(Sips his coffee,...)* But that's the thing though, y'know? Then and now, it's the same thing; 'cept one's cool and the other's stigmatized.

VANESSA: Whata' y'mean?

VIN: Addicts, alcoholics, they're like revered by comparison.

VANESSA: Compared to fat people, y'mean?

VIN: Hell, yeah. Are you kiddin'? Especially to people that don't have a clue. It's like...exotic. They think, like, it takes a special type a' person t'be a drunk or an addict. Great musicians n'poets... *They're* drunks n'addicts. But *anyone* can be fat, so no one wants t'be around 'em. People wana' hang around Keith Richards and Kurt Cobain, not fuckin' John Candy. Y'see? That's what *I* was thinkin' too

VANESSA: Yeah?

VIN: Yeah, I mean, I felt all the same shit that my mother did. I felt depressed, I felt all this, but I knew I'd never get laid if I put all that into food. If I drank, hey, I could meet someone in a bar; a chick who likes bad boys, y'know? It's not like they ain't a dime a' dozen. n'for a while it was okay, but then things start happenin'. Ya' lose friends, ya' lose relationships, your license... Hey, you lost your job. You know about all this.

VANESSA: Wait, I didn't lose my job 'cause a' that.

VIN: Y'didn't?

VANESSA: No. They were cuttin' back, so I was cut.

VIN: You said you were late to work a few times.

VANESSA; Yeah, but that was before I stopped. I didn't say that was why I got let go.

VIN: Alright, but don't you think if you hadn't been late 'cause you were hungover, you mighta' not been expendable ...?

VANESSA: I jus' said it wasn't jus' me, Vin. It was a lay-off. There were others.

VIN: Y'sure?

VANESSA: Yeah, I'm... Look, Vin, I know what I am, okay? But I know why I was let go too, n'it's not cause a' what you think.

VIN: Vanessa, I hate t'say it but denial is...

VANESSA: *(Over "denial is...")* Vin, I don't need to hear the one about the river in Egypt, okay? Now I was fine t'hang with you n'all, but don't start this. I was laid off. Shit happens.

VIN: *(Slight pause.)* Hey, sorry. You're right. Didn't mean to assume anything. Jus' wanted to cheer ya' up, that's all.

VANESSA: Cheer me up? For 30 minutes you're talkin' about how your mother died a slow death for most a' her life, n'that's s'pposed to make me smile?

VIN: Hey, it did, didn't it?

VANESSA: *(She attempts to resist laughing, but slightly slips...)* Yeah, but...

VIN; Y'see?

VANESSA: It's only the way you tell it. It's not at your mother.

VIN: Yeah, whatever.

VANESSA; Vin, I'm not cruel like that. I feel awful for her.

VIN: Hey, there's enough to feel awful about. Let's change the subject then, okay?

(VIN raises cup for waiter, fruitlessly...)

VANESSA; Why'd you feel you needed to cheer me up?

VIN: Whata' y'mean? You're only 2 months sober n'you jus' lost your job.

VANESSA: People lose their jobs. It's not the end a' the world.

VIN: And it's January. I mean, c'mon.

VANESSA; Y'mean New Year's?

76

VIN: Of course New Year's. January. 2017, all that. It's depressing.

VANESSA: Kinda'.

VIN: Nah, it's worse than that. It's one month that never gets easier. Another year, *will it be better? Will it be worse?* Whatcha' didn't accomplish, what *can* ya' accomplish... Everything is flying by ya', and you feel you're jus' sittin' there makin' up for the time you wasted. Kids are becomin' adults too quick, everyone's gettin' famous for the wrong reasons, assholes are becomin' presidents...

VANESSA: It's fucked up.

VIN; I mean, what the...?! I can't even begin t'...

VANESSA: I know.

VIN: I mean 4 years ago I was too wasted to even register, n'here I make it all the way down to the polls, n'*this* is the result?

VANESSA: Hey, he didn't win in New York. We did our job.

VIN; So much for doin' our job.

VANESSA; Jus' sayin'...

VIN; They're all pricks anyway. She wouldnta' been much better.

VANESSA: What?!

VIN: C'mon, V...

VANESSA: She woulda' been *a lot* better, Vin...

VIN: *(Over "Vin...")* Nah, she's as full a' shit as he is.

VANESSA: Vin, c'mon...

VIN: *(Over "c'mon...")* Trust me, she's full of it, V. She jus' disguised it better. Believe me.

VANESSA: And I think you're wrong.

VIN: How do you know I'm wrong?

VANESSA: I didn't say I "know" you're wrong. I said I *think* you're wrong.

VIN: Whatever.

VANESSA: Yeah, whatever.

VIN: *(Sips coffee...)* But y'know, for years, it was like, these people don't represent me. None of 'em. But yet when y'feel better, y'wana go down n' assert yourself, y'know? I mean, we pay taxes. We gotta' fuckin' say, Vanessa.

VANESSA: I know.

VIN: Right? Except it's all bullshit. So here we are. Another year. Another bullshit-artist bein' sworn in. *(Sips coffee, broods...)* Same shit. Maybe even worse.

VANESSA: *(A beat, grins.)* You sure your plan was to cheer me up?

(VIN looks at VANESSA, his struggle is apparent...)

VIN: Y'know what, ...you're right. I better split.
        (...rises...)

VANESSA: Where y'goin', Vin? I thought we were havin' coffee…

VIN: Nah, that's okay. I thought I was helpin' ya', but I'm not doin' such a good job…

VANESSA: Vin, I didn't ask for help, okay? You don't have to do anything here but shoot the shit and have a donut…

VIN: *(Over "have a donut…")* Look, I'm older than you, okay? n'I got almost 5 months a' Goddamn sobriety…!

VANESSA: Vin, take it easy, okay…?

VIN: *(Over "okay…?")* ALMOST 5 MONTHS SOBRIETY, OKAY?!!! YOU ONLY GOT TWO! THAT'S A FUCKIN' CAKEWALK!!! AND Y'WANA ENLIGHTEN **ME**, F'GODSAKES?!!!

> *(VANESSA restrains, looks around, then down at the table… A moment.)*

VANESSA: Vin,…I'm not doin' anything but sittin' here, okay? Y'wana' go, go.

> *(VIN takes a moment, looks around, a bit self-conscious, before sitting…)*

> *(A considerable moment, as Vanessa appears uncomfortable and yet has a compulsion to fill the air…)*

You're right. January sucks. It's like every time you blink now, that ball is slidin' down and that fuckin' blond mimbo Ryan Seacrest is narratin' the end of another year …and you see all these lights and all this money and all this bullshit that goes into all this…bullshit…and you're home on your couch and ya' feel… Jus'… Used to be just a good excuse t'get wasted and

now it jus'…makes you wana' get wasted on all the other days too.
>   *(Slight pause, a grin)*
See, now I'm cheerin' *you* up. See, I turned the tables on ya', Sunshine!

>   *(VIN begrudgingly smiles, but it's brief. They remain, gazing off.)*

VANESSA: Hey, y'know, January ain't all bad though. You know what I read recently? This is some wild shit. January 30th is World Leprosy Day. D'you believe that shit? World Leprosy Day? That's like…I mean, that's like celebratin' hemorrhoids or some shit. *World Leprosy Day?* You ever hearda' this?

>   *(VIN shakes his head "No".)*

I mean, I thought someone misspelled Literacy or somethin', but yeah, there's 'is day that was founded by this French dude in the 50s to acknowledge, like, people who had the disease.

VIN: *(Slight pause.)* What happens? They have, like, a leper parade or somethin'?

VANESSA: I don't think they do much of anything. They just, like, acknowledge that it exists, I guess.

VIN: Why the hell do they do that?

VANESSA: *(Shrugs, slight pause.)* Guess they jus' wana' re-mind people that it's still around n', I dunno', maybe if there's a coupla' alcoholics sittin' around a booth somewhere, bitchin' about the new year, it's a good way to remind 'em that, hey, things may suck at the moment, but…at least they don't have leprosy.

(VIN looks at VANESSA, not sure whether to laugh or admire her wisdom. He picks up his cup and gently clinks hers, then stares out...)

VIN: Sorry I yelled like that. That's not...

VANESSA: It's cool, Vin...

VIN: That's not what I usually...

VANESSA: (Over *"usually..."*) Vin, it's cool. Don't worry about it.

VIN: I guess I've wanted to go off in there a few times and jus'...didn't think it was worth it. They're all so fuckin' self-righteous, y'know? You're the only one I felt was on the same page with me.

VANESSA: Me too.

VIN: I mean, I respect 'em all but, God, bein' around 'em is like a family reunion from hell. Is 'at bad t'say?

VANESSA: Who cares if it is? You're right.

(They share a laugh, which fades after a bit...)

VIN: Sometimes I feel like a leper in *there*, y'know? It's like they're accomplishin' this'n that n'I'm jus' tryin' t'stay afloat. I mean, 5 months ain't exactly a walk in the park. *(Slight pause, a weak laugh.)* But God bless ya', Vanessa. You're doin' good, all things considered. Got your gold chip. 2 months, hey. You're in better shape than I was. Jus' keep doin' it. Good f'you.

(They gaze out, VANESSA is more pensive now. VIN eventually reminds the unseen waitress...)

VIN: *(Internally, as he points to his cup)* Hello? Still here. It's not like we're not payin'.

> *(VIN notices VANESSA's sudden seriousness, as she looks at the gold coin that's been in her hand...)*

VIN: You okay?

VANESSA: *(Pause, unable to look at him.)* Vin?

VIN: Yeah?

VANESSA: *(Slight pause, barely containing...)* Vin...?

VIN: What is it? Tell me. What's up...?

VANESSA: *(Over "What's up...?")* **I fell off.**

VIN: *(A beat.)* What?

VANESSA: *(Pause.)* Had my annual review with my manager. I thought I was doin' ok there, y'know? I mean, it ain't like I loved being there, but I thought I was at least doin' well enough. He gave me shit fa' somethin'. Mighta' not even been as bad as I thought, but... Tells me what my Christmas bonus was, which was shit compared to what I thought I... I mean, I could barely live off that job, y'know? So he finishes his review. Asks me if I have any questions. But I just sat there. I couldn't think of anything, like, intelligent to say. So I didn't say anything. Left his office. Went t'lunch. *(Slight pause.)* Had a few, came back - cursed 'im out in fronta' everyone, Vin. *Everyone. (Slight pause.)* So that's why I was...

> *(A moment, as they remain still. VANESSA looking out, VIN looking at her.)*

VIN: Hey,...it's okay.

VANESSA: I fucked up.

VIN: It's okay.

VANESSA: I fucked up bad, Vin... I really... Shit...

> *(VANESSA is about to cry, but restrains, smiles, ...takes a sip, looks out, but remains frail, as VIN observes her.)*

VIN: Hey,...it's cool. You're here, okay? And I'm here. So..., y'know,... *(Slight pause.)* We got all night. I ain't goin' anywhere. Okay?

> *(VANESSA reluctantly nods... A beat.)*

Let's get some pie. Okay? I got my eye on that apple one.

> *(VIN's grin brings a reluctant one to VANESSA.)*

VIN: Ala mode with like a brownie on top. Let's live a little, alright? What the hell. Sound good?

> *(After a beat, VANESSA nods.)*

Cool.

> *(They look at each other for a moment...)*

> *(Lights Fade.)*

End of Play

STAY

STAY

STAY received its World Premiere as part of Brass Tacks Theater Company's 2nd Annual Rosetta Festival of New Works in April 2003 at the Creative Place Theatre in New York City, with the following cast and director:

GUY……….………….……..Andy Girard

GILBERT……………….…..…Matt Walters

Directed by Laura Schutzel

Artistic Directors: Melinda Ferraraccio and Kevin Molesworth

STAY was subsequently revived in 2009 at Where Eagles Dare Theatre in NYC , and as part of *The World is My Cheesecake*, an Evening of Short Plays by Daniel Damiano, produced by Mind The Gap Theatre Company and fandango 4 productions, September 2011, in New York City: both productions featured DH Johnson as Guy and George Stavropoulos as Gil, and were Directed by the Author.

Cast of Characters

GUY - *Initially overbearing, 30's-40's.*

GILBERT - *Initially obliging, 30's-40's (but should not look older than GUY.)*

The play takes place in a café, of sorts.

The Time is the Present.

STAY

*GUY and GILBERT sit across from each
other at a small, bare table…*

GUY: As I was saying… By the way, do you like Devil Dogs?

GILBERT: Devil what?

GUY: Devil Dogs? Chocolate devil's food cake sandwiching a deliciously creamy substance?

GILBERT: *(Oddly.)* Uh…well, I'm…

GUY: Just incredible.

GILBERT: Uh, yes…I suppose they…

GUY: Aren't they?

GILBERT: I…yes, mhm.

GUY: Anyway, as I was saying… My God, it's chilly in here, isn't it?

GILBERT: *(Not mutual.)* Well,…

GUY: I should've worn my cardigan, only I hate to be perceived as a yuppy.

GILBERT: I'm sorry?

GUY: You know, a yuppy with a sweater and a rich father.

GILBERT: *(Slight pause.)* I don't see the connection.

GUY: You don't.

GILBERT: I'm afraid not.

GUY: Really?

GILBERT: *(Gingerly.)* Really.

GUY: *(Thinks.)* Hm. Maybe I *should've* worn it.

GILBERT: *(Slight pause.)* Would you like to go somewhere else?

GUY: *(Abrupt and grand...)* No, no, this'll do fine! I'd rather stay in one place so as to maintain my focus, as I have something very important to say.

GILBERT: *(Pleasantly eager.)* Alright.

GUY: So, as I was saying...

GILBERT: Yes?

GUY: Oop, you threw me.

GILBERT: I'm...I'm sorry?

GUY: *(A condescending grin.)* I wasn't expecting a response.

GILBERT: Oh.

GUY: Let's try this again...

GILBERT: Okay.

GUY: Oop, you threw me again.

GILBERT: Did I?

GUY: Yes. I'm sorry, would you be kind enough to let me complete my thought?

(GILBERT reluctantly does not respond.)

Would you?!

GILBERT: *(Tentatively.)* Should I respond?

GUY: Well, of course. Better than just sit there.

GILBERT: Well, I wasn't sure if a response would throw you.

GUY: Why would it throw me?

GILBERT: Well, I mean, with all due respect, we've been here for 20 minutes and I'm still waiting to hear what you have to say.

GUY: Are you finished?

GILBERT: Uh...

GUY: Good. Now as I was saying... I'm sorry, would you mind not hunching?

GILBERT: Not what?

GUY: Hunching. Your back. You look as if you're about to excrete.

GILBERT: *(Somewhat embarrassed.)* Oh, al...alright.

(...as GILBERT aligns himself.)

GUY: Much better.

GILBERT: Is it?

GUY: It is. So, as I was saying... By the way, I apologize if what I said appeared insensitive.

GILBERT: About my posture?

GUY: About your breath.

GILBERT: My breath?!

GUY: Yes.

GILBERT: You didn't say... My breath is bad?

GUY: Almost evil. In any case, I was...

      (...as GILBERT motions to his pocket...)

What the hell are you doing?

GILBERT: I'm...getting gum.

GUY: Why?

GILBERT: To refresh my breath.

GUY: Do you feel the need?

GILBERT: Well, apparently...

GUY: Can you please stop?

GILBERT: What?

GUY: Stop getting gum, please.

GILBERT: I don't see why pulling out a stick of gum should throw you.

GUY: *(Suddenly incensed.)* You **wouldn't** see it, would you. You wouldn't see how **any**thing that you do could "throw me".

90

The gum, the breath, the posture, your verbal interruptions. Your perpetual flatulence!

GILBERT: **Flatulence?!**

GUY: Yes, flatulence! My God, it's like having a conversation with a whoopee cushion.

GILBERT: Look, I don't know what you're hearing but it certainly isn't coming from *me*.

GUY: Oh, yes. That's what they **all** say, as they leave with a hole burned into the ass of their pants.

GILBERT: You know, I think there's something wrong with you.

GUY: Something wrong with **me**?!

GILBERT: *(Rises...)* Look, I'm a very busy person, alright?

GUY: As am I.

GILBERT: Well, you invited me here because you claimed that you had something "important" to tell me.

GUY: I do.

GILBERT: Well, what is it?

GUY: There's no need to...

GILBERT: I am very pressed for time, do you understand?!

GUY: *(Slight pause, conceding.)* I understand. Please,...sit.

(GILBERT sits, reluctantly.)

Now, as I was saying…

(A long, empty moment, as GUY remains still…before, finally…)

GILBERT: **Yes?!**

GUY: Oop, you threw me again.

GILBERT: Alright, that's it.

GUY: What?

(…as GILBERT rises…)

GILBERT: You don't have a thing to tell me. I think you're just someone who relishes abusing others to compensate for your own lack of substance.

GUY: That couldn't be further from the truth.

GILBERT: Well, I don't care what you think. I don't even know you, for Godsakes.

GUY: All the more reason not to rush to judgment.

GILBERT: I'm leaving.

(GILBERT motions to exit, GUY rises…)

GUY: *(Suddenly desperate.)* Don't go!

GILBERT: *(Stops.)* Why the hell should I stay?

GUY: *(Attempting to compose.)* I…I…I have something important to say.

GILBERT: *(Incredulous.)* You do.

GUY: Yes, I do.

GILBERT: What?

(A moment. GUY is awkward.)

What?!!!

GUY: *(Grasping.)* Well, I…I…I…

GILBERT: Goodbye.

(GILBERT motions to leave…)

GUY: MY MOTHER WAS A PROSTITUTE!!!

(GILBERT stops.)

(A moment.)

GILBERT: What?

GUY: Yes. A lady of the evening. I was raised amidst a swarm of…of…of…

GILBERT: What?

GUY: Those men.

GILBERT: What men?

GUY: The men who pay prostitutes.

GILBERT: Johns?

GUY: **Johns!** Yes, Johns! Oh, God, **Johns** everywhere! And the alcohol.

GILBERT: Your mother was an alcoholic?

GUY: She was when she wasn't doing heroin.

GILBERT: Oh, my.

GUY: Cocaine.

GILBERT: Oh, God!

GUY: CRACK!

GILBERT: NO!

GUY: YES!

GILBERT: Where was your father?

GUY: *(Dramatic pause.)* My…my father died when I was 12.

GILBERT: I'm so sorry.

GUY: He choked.

GILBERT: That's awful.

GUY: On a Devil Dog.

GILBERT: My God!

GUY: I felt so guilty.

GILBERT: Why?

GUY: *(Near tears, grandly.)* I DRANK ALL THE MILK!

GILBERT: Oh, shit.

GUY: There I stood over him, innocently eating a bowl of Life cereal as my father turned blue.

GILBERT: Tsch.

> *(They both look out, absorbed by the intensity of the story. A moment.)*

GILBERT: *(In thought.)* How ironic.

GUY: *(Slight pause.)* What?

GILBERT: That you were eating Life…as your father died.

GUY: *(Gradually connecting.)* Yes, that…that *is* ironic, isn't it. Well, be that as it may, that's…what happened.

> *(GUY sits, seemingly despondent.)*

GILBERT: *(Pensively.)* God.

GUY: *(Milking slightly.)* Yes.

GILBERT: Just terrible.

GUY: It was.

GILBERT: You must be…

GUY: I am.

GILBERT: I figured.

GUY: Yes.

GILBERT: I'm sorry.

GUY: It's not any fault of yours.

GILBERT: I mean, about…before.

GUY: Oh, please. Think nothing of it.

GILBERT: *(Slight pause, delicately.)* Was that what you wanted to tell me?

GUY: Uh…no, actually. That all just slipped out inadvertently.

GILBERT: So you…still have that important thing to tell me then.

GUY: *(Feigning courtesy.)* Actually, I do but…I'm sure you have better things to do.

(A moment, before GILBERT sits, gladly.)

GILBERT: I'm looking forward to it.

GUY: You're sure I'm not keeping you?

GILBERT: *(Looks at watch.)* Well, I do have some pressing engagements in a bit but…I'd still like to hear what you have to say.

GUY: How nice of you.

GILBERT: My pleasure.

GUY: *(Jovially.)* So where were we before I digressed? Ah, yes! As I was saying… By the way, would you mind not doing that?

GILBERT: Doing what?

GUY: With your tongue.

GILBERT: Doing what with my tongue?

GUY: Clucking.

GILBERT: Clucking?

GUY: It sounds like a ping-pong game going on inside of your mouth.

GILBERT: I'm sorry, I wasn't aware that I was…

GUY: Thank you. Now, as I was saying…

GILBERT: Wait a second.

GUY: Oop, you threw me again.

GILBERT: Bullshit!

GUY: Excuse me?

GILBERT: I was making no such sounds.

GUY: I'm afraid you were…

GILBERT: No, I wasn't!

GUY: Yes, you were.

(GILBERT rises…)

GILBERT: Look, you're either trying to make me crazy or you really are so desperate for someone to unleash your mind games on that you'll resort to anything to contain them.

GUY: Like what?

GILBERT: Creating a tragic childhood!

GUY: Creating?!

GILBERT: An alcoholic, drug-addicted, prostitute mother?!

GUY: *(Weakening slightly.)* She was.

GILBERT: A father who choked to death on a Devil Dog?!

GUY: It's true!

GILBERT: As "true" as my clucking?! My bad breath?! My perpetual farting?!!!

GUY: Yes!

GILBERT: You are a fucking madman! This is the first and last time that I will waste a second of my life in your presence, do you understand?! I've done nothing that you allege. My God, with all that's happened in the world, with all the pain, the anguish, the suffering…and you have nothing better to do than seek out people who you feel you can deceive to your black heart's content! I've just sat here, stupidly, while you've blatantly wasted my time. Taken minutes from my life that I will never see again. Well, find another victim because I'm through! Do you hear me?! I'll leave you to yourself, the greatest pain that I can inflict on you.

> *(As GUY wipes his eyes…)*

Oh, that's right, wipe your "tears". I'm sure you're emotionally stricken by what I've just said.

GUY: No, you're spitting in my face. My God, say it, don't spray it.

GILBERT: GO TO HELL!

GUY: He says, as he continues to fart through the alphabet.

GILBERT: How dare you!

GUY: Yes, it's quite a talent you have there.

GILBERT: I AM NOT FARTING!!!

GUY: Tell that to the chair.

GILBERT: You are certifiable.

GUY: No, just honest. A little less denial would bode well for your future relationships.

GILBERT: You're unbelievable.

GUY: Only to those who refuse to believe.

GILBERT: And we don't have a relationship! We just met a half hour ago! We're not friends of any kind, do you understand?!!!

GUY: *(Pause, visibly stung.)* I…I suppose that's true.

GILBERT: It *is* true!

GUY: *(Vulnerably…)* So…you won't stay?

GILBERT: No, I won't. Not a second more.

(GILBERT motions to leave, then stops, turns…
and rapidly…)

I have a life! I have people to see, places to go, things to do. I have friends! People who actually enjoy my company. Who interact with me in an emotionally nourishing way!

(GILBERT motions to leave, then stops, turns…)

99

I have a family who adores me! A father, a mother, a sister, a brother. All of whom are always eager to hear about my very exciting life: my adventures, travels, etc!

(GILBERT motions to leave, then stops, turns…)

I have a gorgeous girlfriend who loves me more than life and can't wait to see me, to kiss me, to grope me as if I were a greased-up Chippendale dancer! I have a public that awaits my presence whenever I can spare it and yet I've been gracious enough to give an hour of my valuable time to *you*; A delusional imbecile who can't distinguish between fantasy and reality! A PSYCHOPATH who hears clucks and farts like others breathe!

(GILBERT motions, before maniacally…)

NO, I WILL NOT "STAY"! NOT A SECOND MORE! NOT A SECOND MORE, DO YOU HEAR ME?! **I – AM – LEAVING!!!!!**

(They are both still for a considerable moment. GILBERT panting heavily while GUY somberly looks out…)

GUY: I envy you.

GILBERT: *(Offguarded, then smugly.)* As…as well you should.

GUY: There is nothing as important as being wanted. Loved. But not everyone is as fortunate. Yet…here you are.

GILBERT: *(Bogusly.)* Yes, well.

GUY: I do thank you for the time that you've spared for me.

GILBERT: *(Slight pause.)* Yes, well.

(A still moment.)

GUY: *(Sadly, sincerely.)* I suppose you'll be going.

GILBERT: *(Feigned urgency.)* Yes, I must.

GUY: All the best to you.

GILBERT: Thank you.

GUY: You're welcome.

GILBERT: Many...urgent matters to attend to.

GUY: I'm sure.

GILBERT: Yes.

GUY: Yes.

GILBERT: *(Slight pause, emptily...)* Yes.

> *(They remain silent and still for a lengthy moment...before GILBERT slowly and ashamedly goes back to chair and sits. He looks out, hopelessly.)*

> *(GUY observes this for a moment, as he gradually forms a slight but desperate grin.)*

GUY: *(A weak though animated snicker.)* It's a shame.

GILBERT: *(Slight pause, sadly elsewhere.)* It is.

GUY: *(Slight pause, obviously grasping.)* I mean, that...I forgot what important thing I had to tell you.

GILBERT: *(Slight pause, near tears.)* It doesn't matter.

(GUY looks over at GILBERT, somewhat taken aback by his candor, before facing out again...)

GUY: *(Slight pause, reluctantly but, at last, admittedly...)* No, ...I...I suppose it doesn't.

(They continue to gaze out austerely...as the lights fade out...)

End of Play

THE KING OF SOMETHING

THE KING OF SOMETHING

The King of Something was presented as a Zoom Reading as part of fandango 4 Art House's Snippet Theatre Series, April 2020, with the following cast and director:

KING……………………………..John Blaylock
TOWNSWOMAN #1……………Brooke Turner
TOWNSMAN #1….Christopher Romero Wilson
TOWNSWOMAN #2………………..Kate Greer
TOWNSMAN #2………………….Eric Percival

Directed by the Author

Artistic Directors: Judy Alvarez and Daniel Damiano

Cast of Characters

KING – *Somewhat small in stature, 50s.*

TOWNSMAN #1 – *A local citizen, 30s-40s.*

TOWNSMAN #2 – *A local citizen, 30s-40s.*

TOWNSWOMAN #1- *A local citizen, 30s-40s.*

TOWNSWOMAN #2 – *A local citizen, 30s-40s.*

England.

The 1600s (or thereabouts).

A Town Square.

*The KING sits on a throne, adorned in crown, robe, with sword
in hand, as Townsman #1 and 2 and Townswoman #1 and 2
observe.*

KING: I am King, I am King - and not just for a mere day,
for I am royalty incarnate, in the flesh that's on display.
I am King, I am King – I say with most unbridled force,
with head of crown, clad in robe, and authority, of course.
I am King, I am King, for England's living and it's dead,
for whom I've waged through endless battles and copious
bloodshed.
Surviving all to rule and to most righteously lead,
for the good people of Old England, for which I forever
bleed.

MAN #1: Could that be His Majesty upon that chair?

WOMAN #1: Bereft of guards, out in the open air?

MAN #2: Why, his adornments are enough to make it clear.

WOMAN #2: Though his proclamations are most dubious, I
fear.

WOMAN #1: I'd wager he's not the king,
but a man with a crown;
one he could've purchased with sole intent to astound.

MAN #2: He is king, thrice said, despite your fervent audacity;
can you not feel the tremors of his emphatic royalty?

WOMAN #2: Is that what that is? I thought it might be the
wind,
passing briskly through his robe of deep crimson.

WOMAN #1: Pardon me, sir, but are you in fact the king?!

MAN #2: Pray, woman, are you mad?! You dare ask such a thing?!

WOMAN #1: Well, how should one know if one doesn't inquire?

MAN #2: Why, is a swift mortality something you desire?
She speaks not for the rest, Your Highness.
Therefore, we beg your disregard.

WOMAN #2: You needn't speak for me, good sir,
for my clarity's most on par.

MAN #1: One has every right to doubt, when such an assertion is made,
for it takes more than *"I am King"* to easily persuade.

KING: Now, now, good people – I'm not one for a violent stand,
for this good king has chosen to rule with a softer hand.
Therefore, if the merit of my claim has yet to've taken flight,
I will grant each of you one query, in proof that I am right.

MAN #1: Very well, sir. In case you are, in fact, the king,
might I commend your open mind, to allow such questioning.

MAN #2: I don't question him at all. Why, he's the king,
as clear as day.

KING: Bless you, my dear man. You'll be my heir apparent,
I say.

MAN #2: Bless you, your highness. I accept what you'll bestow.

WOMAN#1: And yet there's still much information for us to know.

WOMAN #2: My question to you, if you are indeed king,
as you allege;
how did you become king, and to what allegiance do you
pledge?

KING: God is my allegiance, and I am king as kings are such;
through tireless toil and battling much.

MAN #1: In what battles did you engage in, and what injuries
did you acquire?

KING: The Battle of Battles, the War of Wars,
and several wounds, from sword and fire.

WOMAN #1: On what areas are these scars that you speak so
proudly of?

KING: Why, here, there and everywhere, all over and above.

WOMAN #2: Well, sir, that's most enlightening, but kindly, if
you would,
elaborate to some degree so that it's clearly understood.

KING: *(Rises, then...)*
An impaled pectoral, an impeded rump,
a gouged left eye, and a right wooden stump,
a deviated septum, and a garroted spleen,
a split to the chin, and a case of gangrene
a throat well-sliced, and scalp well shaved,
a severed left sternum, and a knee ill-behaved
an elasticized hip, and a wonky right eye,
a dose of the plague, with a twist of a sty.

MAN #2: Most impressive, your highness. There, there.
Now, you see?
This man has fought for England, and led us valiantly.

WOMAN #1: Yet heretofore he's been unseen, unrecognizable to all,
which is why he can be anyone, creating tales miles tall.

WOMAN #2: I've never heard of the Battle of Battles,
nor the War of Wars.
Why, what if the only battle he's fought is the hoisting
of his drawers?

MAN #2: What more do you ask of him?! For the man has given blood and bone,

KING: which has more than earned my ascension to this considerable throne.

MAN #2: He's sacrificed his very life, endured myriad attacks…

KING: Why, for the good of great England, I've collapsed my very BACK…!

(The King clutches his chest on the last word…)

MAN #2: Your Highness…

KING: God has clenched my heart with might...

(ALL OTHERS GASP!)

KING: My breath is fleeting, an unyielding plight...

(ALL OTHERS GASP LOUDER…!)

KING: Angels escort me to the blinding light…!

(ALL OTHERS GASP LOUDER…!)

(The KING collapses off of his throne and onto the platform with a resounding thud!)

(MAN #1 urgently feels his pulse…)

MAN #1: Alas, his majesty has lost this fight.

(A moment.)

WOMAN #2: His flesh remains aground, while his noble spirit has fled,

MAN #1: a dark day for England, indeed,…

MAN #1, WOMAN #1 & 2: for the good king is now…dead.

MAN #2: Oh, now it's credence you give in time for our majesty's demise.
Whereas in life, you filled his air with cynicism, unwise.

MAN #1: I'm afraid a face unbeknownst to a veritable some, suddenly becomes king in death's wisdom.

WOMAN #1: And now that he's passed, it somehow seems that it were true;

WOMAN #2: he was indeed our loyal king,…despite our skeptical view.

(As Man #2 proceeds to undress the dead king, as he righteously speaks…)

MAN #2: Well, how noble of you to possess such hindsight, whereas I always believed him utterly and outright.
I saw in him bravery, a ruler's passion in his heart, and remained undaunted, due in no small part
to my belief that a man is what he claims to be, be it a king, a czar or such sovereignty.

110

Therefore, my reward for loyalty is my ascension to his throne.
Believe in my dominion, and you will not be alone.

>*(MAN #2 stands in full king regalia, now as KING #2,*
>*as the dead, nearly-naked KING #1 rolls off platform*
>*and thuds onto the street...)*

>*(A moment.)*

WOMAN #1: I suppose we've little choice, if we believed the
dead one now as king.

WOMAN #2: For he did name this one as heir, or some such
thing.

MAN #1: Well, while the dead king's claims may well have
been true,
may you at least provide substance for our worshipping *you*?

KING #2: How dare you doubt my words – for they are more
than enough!
Your insolence an insult for suggesting a royal bluff!

MAN #1: But...

KING #2: I am King! – I am King! – do you hear me clear?!
He said I was his heir apparent, for all of you to hear.
That means I have the power, that it is I who reigns,
and if you dare doubt my imposing stature, I'll reduce you to
a stain!

>*(ALL OTHERS GASP!)*

WOMAN #1: Such brutality! Is that an act that you espouse?!
Because he merely is uncertain, you will punish for his doubts?

WOMAN #2: This is how you allege to rule? With intolerance
and rage?

111

MAN #1: Can't one merely pose a question, at this rather early stage?

KING #2: I'm not here to indulge queries! That's not how a king should rule!

WOMAN #2: But *he* allowed them from all of us.

KING #2: *(Rises...)*
AND THAT'S BECAUSE HE WAS A FOOL!

> *(ALL OTHERS GASP!)*

MAN #1: You say this about a man who was once your king as well?

WOMAN #2: Who gave you your ascension just before his death knell?

KING #2: SILENCE, AT ONCE, I SAY! For his death,
I cannot be blamed!
I am your majesty! Your Highness! And other ennobling names!
It was you who broke his heart, which led to his demise;
you questioned his very being, and he was not very wise
to indulge you with his answers, for no king need defend
what they've done or what they did, which allowed them
to ascend.
He was king and now he's dead, and so he's passed his crown to me
and so here I stand before you, the very height of regality.
In closing, I demand only that you worship me, your King,
that you love me more than life, and forego all questioning!

> *(KING # 2 sits. MAN#1, WOMAN #1 & 2 kneel*
> *reluctantly before him...)*

MAN #1: My apologies for challenging your majesty's esteem.

WOMAN #2: Insulting our good king is something we dare would not dream.

WOMAN #1: Forgive our transgressions, and let us worship, as you desire.

MAN #1: *(Rises...)*
Though before we do, your majesty, might I once more inquire...?

KING #2: Sit down, you fool, have I not made myself clear?! This is not a democracy that I'm overseeing here!!!

> *(MAN #1 approaches the barely dressed dead king...)*

MAN #1: Nevertheless, I'm afraid that something is askew! The dead king had claimed injuries that fail to be in view!

> *(As the Women rise, Man #1 stands the dead King up right, as he manipulates him like a marionette through out the following...)*

He doesn't have a split chin,

WOMAN #1: nor an impeded rump,

WOMAN #2: nor a garroted spleen,

MAN #1: nor a right wooden stump.

WOMAN #1: nor a throat well-sliced,

WOMAN #2: nor a gouged left-eye,

MAN #1: nor an impaled pectoral,

ALL but KING #2: **Why, it's all been a lie!**

(The dead King falls lifeless to the floor again, with a resounding thud! They gaze at KING #2 skeptically, before he rises...)

KING #2: And there you have the reason for our most shameful state;
a country I must rescue from a fool who met his fate.
What a pity for he to leave this earth with a legacy of lies;
an open-minded man, you thought, who cared only to defy.
Yet how fortunate you are, to have such a king as this,
who commands your undying worship, and who will rule with an iron fist!

WOMAN #1: And to you, ol' good "King", we say, enjoy the view from your throne,
However, I think you'll find a draft, for you will find yourself alone.

KING #2: What? What? Wait! Wait! I haven't ordered you to leave!
For I am still your king, despite the tricks up a dead man's sleeve.
You will ask not my motives, and do all that I require,
for God has bestowed upon you an unyielding empire!

MAN#1: God took a mere man to the clouds, who had no further business here,
and so you've taken it upon yourself to impose a ruse of fear.

WOMAN #1: Coercing us to believe that you are something of a sort,
with shiny crown and glossy robe, and a majesty's retort.

WOMAN # 2: But it all amounts to little, a mere expression of gall,
for a foolish man there and his newly appointed heir…

MAN #1, WOMAN #1 & 2: **were never kings, at all.**

(They leave, as KING #2 remains, aghast...)

KING #2: I...I...I say I am King! I AM KING! –
AND NOTHING ELSE NEED BE SAID,
FOR MY WRATH WILL SOON BE UPON YOU ALL –
AND SEVER YOUR MEAGER HEADS!

(He awaits for their return, before more desperately...)

Why, you'll...YOU'LL REGRET THIS ACT OF TREASON,
YOUR BETRAYAL OF YOUR KIIIIING!!!!!
(internally) If not necessarily that of England,
then certainly not...nothing?

> *(He sits dejectedly with sword in hand for a moment, be-*
> *fore slowly removing his crown and robe, and placing*
> *them upon the throne, leaning sword against it. Once*
> *again, he is Man #2.)*

> *(As he gradually, and defeatedly, steps down from plat*
> *form, he catches further glimpse of the dead "King"...)*

MAN #2: Upon further glance, sans crown,...I now recall
your face.
Not a man of even vague esteem, but a beggar out of place.
I've often seen you pilfering fruit or discarded in the street,
a ne'er do well whom misfortune befell, with old shoes upon
your feet.
Somehow you came upon these toys for your elaborate façade,
Claiming yourself as king and pledging allegiance to God.
I can only hope he's with you now, and greets you not
with shame,
but admiration for your attempt at being what none of us
can claim.
At least your grand delusions rendered you a king of good
intent,
whereas my violent scheme for my fatuous regime was merely
fire spent.

Therefore, for what little it's worth, I bestow upon you these things,
that may not render you King of England…but perhaps…
King of *something*.

    (Man #2 places the robe upon the dead man, then gently the crown, then places the sword in his lifeless grip.)

    (He then kneels, gives the sign of the cross, as the others come back on, having overheard this. They do the same,…then remain on one knee - still.)

    (Lights fade…)

End of Play

A MOMENT OF WEAKNESS

A MOMENT OF WEAKNESS

A Moment of Weakness received its World Premiere as part of Pulse Ensemble Theatre's One-Act Festival in December 2000 in New York City, with the following cast and director:

LAURA.........................Judy Alvarez
WOMAN.........................Ann Parker

Directed by Kathleen Kerns

Artistic Director: Alexa Kelly

A Moment of Weakness was subsequently revived as part of *The World is My Cheesecake*, an Evening of One-Act Plays by Daniel Damiano, produced by Mind The Gap Theatre Company and fandango 4 productions, September 2011, in New York City, with Judy Alvarez as Laura and Sue Glausen as Woman. Directed by the Author

Cast of Characters

LAURA - *Mid-to-late 30's. Self-reliant. Her personal traits have been predominantly masked by a business-like persona. She is dressed in corporate attire.*

WOMAN - *Late 60's. Earthy, maternal and seemingly genuine.*

A city bus in winter.

Afternoon.

The Time is the Present.

WOMAN and LAURA sit beside each other, facing out. LAURA is currently on her cellular phone, in the midst of speaking...

LAURA: *(Impatient, yet maintaining her exterior.)* It's leaving at 4. I asked for the earliest departure. *(Waits.)* I don't know anything. As I said, my father called and told me they rushed her to the hospital. I have no idea what her status is, the severity... I have no idea. I just threw some stuff in a bag and now I'm on the bus. *(Waits, curtly.)* Well, I didn't have a choice, Brian. There's a taxi strike and I couldn't get a car service soon enough. *(Waits.)* Well, my God, don't you think I'd prefer to *not* be on a bus right now? *(Waits.)* Yes, I'm fine. You asked me that three times already, and I really hate repeating myself, alright? Look, I'm getting close, so let me go, okay? I'll call you when I know something. *(Waits, ...)* Brian, I am fine. *(Waits.)* Bye.

> *(She clicks off phone abruptly and places it inside her purse on her lap. She then pulls out a planner and pensively jots...)*

> *(After a moment, WOMAN subtly turns to LAURA and with great sincerity...)*

WOMAN: Your mother had a stroke.

LAURA: *(Offguardedly turns to her...)* Excuse me?

WOMAN: Your mother had a stroke.

LAURA: *(Curtly, before resuming w/ notations.)* Yes.

WOMAN: *(Slight pause.)* Just happened.

LAURA: *(Slight pause.)* Yes, it did.

WOMAN: How old is she, your mother?

LAURA: I'm sorry?

WOMAN: How old is she?

LAURA: *(Unwilling to commit to an exchange.)* She's 72.

WOMAN: Oh, dear, that's not old.

LAURA: Well, that's her age.

WOMAN: I understand. I'm just saying she's not an old lady…

LAURA: Thank you, yes. Now if you don't mind, I really need…

WOMAN: Oh, I'm sorry. Of course.

LAURA: Thank you.

> *(LAURA looks at watch, before resuming.)*

> *(A moment, as WOMAN looks out.)*

WOMAN: So she's in Florida.

LAURA: *(Slight pause.)* I'm sorry?

WOMAN: She's in Florida? That's where you're going…?

LAURA: Yes.

WOMAN: Oh, good for her. Good air down there,…

LAURA: Mhm.

WOMAN: Sunlight.

LAURA: Mhm.

WOMAN: Oh, yes.

> *(A moment, as LAURA's eyes try to remain on her planner. WOMAN turns back out, ...)*

> *(A moment.)*

WOMAN: She'll be just fine.

LAURA: *(Reluctantly, as she writes...)* She was prior to *this*.

> *(A moment, before WOMAN takes LAURA's hand, prompting LAURA to become somewhat startled...)*

WOMAN: *(With deeper resonance...)* She'll be fine, dear.

LAURA: *(Stunned but somewhat touched, a moment.)* That's...that's very sweet. Thank you...for that.

WOMAN: It's not sweet, darling. *(Pats LAURA's hand.)* And there's nothing to thank me for. Nothing at all. Please.

> *(WOMAN removes her hand while continuing to smile at LAURA, before facing out.)*

> *(LAURA continues to observe WOMAN with some astonishment, ...before gradually going back to planner.)*

> *(A moment...)*

WOMAN: How long has it been since you've seen her?

LAURA: *(Tentatively,...)* A while.

WOMAN: Why so long, if you don't mind me asking?

LAURA: *(Slight pause, awkwardly.)* Well, it's just…
My career takes up a lot of my time.

WOMAN: I see.

LAURA: Mhm.

WOMAN: What do you do?

LAURA: *(Hesitantly,…)* I'm…hired by different companies
to…basically increase morale when there's been sort of a drop
off in performance.

WOMAN: Oh. You help them sort of…get back on track?

LAURA: Pretty much.

WOMAN: You're like a…what do they call it, a motivational
speaker?

LAURA: Yes, exactly.

WOMAN: Look at that.

LAURA: *(A tepid smile.)* Hm.

WOMAN: Well, that's certainly admirable.

LAURA: Oh, well, that's…

WOMAN: Getting employees to raise their standards.

LAURA: Well, it's…

WOMAN: And what a time for that, right?

LAURA: Sure.

WOMAN: With the economy, the unemployment situation…

LAURA: Of course.

WOMAN: You work for yourself?

LAURA: Um…yes. It's my own business.

WOMAN: Well, look at that. How proud your family must be.

LAURA: Well,…

WOMAN: So your job takes you out of town often.

LAURA: Yes. Quite a bit. Mhm.

WOMAN: I see. *(Slight pause.)* That was your husband?

LAURA: *(Offguard, before…)* Yes.

WOMAN: *(A beat, with a grin.)* Any children?

LAURA: In 2 years.

WOMAN: *(A gentle snicker.)* Well.

LAURA: What?

WOMAN: You're very structured.

LAURA: *(A slightly defensive grin.)* Hm.

> *(A moment, as they both look out. Only the faint sounds of traffic,…)*

LAURA: *(Strangely compelled…)* We were gonna' fly down a couple of Christmases ago but there was a blizzard so…the flight was cancelled and…we couldn't reschedule.

WOMAN: And then things got busy for you.

LAURA: *(Slight pause.)* Yeah, they…they did.

WOMAN: You've had bad luck with planes?

LAURA: Well, not… Actually, yeah, now that I think about it. Of late, at least. Delays, cancellations. Yeah. Fortunately, it hasn't cost me work, but…

WOMAN: But I'm sure missing Christmas with your mother was a particular disappointment for you.

> *(LAURA can only display a tepid grin, as WOMAN looks at her, sensing…)*

She'll be fine.

LAURA: *(Again, touched but more indulging.)* I appreciate that. You're very sweet.

WOMAN: Dear, there's nothing to appreciate. It's honesty. Any person has a right to honesty. That's all I'm telling you.

LAURA: *(Slight pause.)* You say it with such conviction. It's…it's as if you *know* this.

WOMAN: *(Smiles.)* Why do you think I'm telling you, dear?

LAURA: *(Slight pause, with incredulity.)* Are you a clairvoy-ant of some kind or…?

WOMAN: No.

LAURA: It's just…what, intuition?

WOMAN: No more than the next person. Sometimes you just get a feeling, like anybody else. You know, like how you can sometimes tell a person's name by their face.

LAURA: Well, *I* can't do that but...

WOMAN: You probably can.

   (LAURA weakly snickers...)

I probably look like a name to you.

LAURA: What *is* your name, if you don't mind me asking?

WOMAN: I don't at all, but why don't you take a guess?

LAURA: *(Slightly offput, then with amused embarrassment...)* Oh, no...that's...

WOMAN: Try.

LAURA: *(Slight pause, with a cautious grin.)* You're just try-ing to make me smile.

WOMAN: You're already smiling, dear.

   (LAURA, finally appeasing, looks into WOMAN's face awkwardly.)

LAURA: Well, you sort of remind me of an aunt that I have. You kind of have her way.

WOMAN: What's her name?

LAURA: Vera.

WOMAN: Really.

LAURA: Is…is that your name?

WOMAN: It is now.

LAURA: No, really. What's your name?

WOMAN: Call me Vera. Yours is Laura, right?

LAURA: *(Taken aback.)* I…yeah, that's… How did you…?
Did…did I say it when I was on the phone?

WOMAN: You may have.

LAURA: *(A beat.)* Huh. I don't remember but… Anyway, it's
nice to meet you,…Vera.

> *(As LAURA holds her hand out somewhat warily.*
> *WOMAN takes a firm hold, they shake…)*

WOMAN: Are you gonna' be alright?

LAURA: Oh, ye…I'm…yes, thank you.

WOMAN: She'll be around this Christmas, trust me. You'll go
down with your husband, see her… It'll be wonderful. It'll be
as if this never happened.

LAURA: Thank you.

WOMAN: Laura, I've told you, it's true. I'm not doing *any*-
thing.

LAURA: Well, just…to have someone say what you're saying…

WOMAN: It'll be fine, dear.

LAURA: I mean, when you're not a doctor and you get this kind of news, you just... You feel...very... It's...it's just not a feeling that I'm used to.

WOMAN: I'm sure.

LAURA: *(Restraining, she grins weakly.)* Hm.

WOMAN: Believe me, it's very frustrating. I lost three husbands.

LAURA: Oh, God.

WOMAN: Mhm. I remember thinking at one point that if I just sat alone in a room and avoided contact with the outside world and didn't get attached to anybody, it'd be the only way that I'd escape misfortune. But, of course, it's silly to think that way.

LAURA: Sure.

WOMAN: Afterall, I could get sick just from sitting in a room.

LAURA: That's...yes, that's true.

WOMAN: I could get sick from *sitting*.

> *(WOMAN laughs boisterously, LAURA eventually snickers along with her...)*

Anyway, you *have* to meet people, you *have* to go outside. Unless you get yourself holed-up inside of an institution, you have to make yourself somehow accessible to all the bad that can happen to you or someone you care about, otherwise what's the purpose of living? There's no way to *always* be prepared.

LAURA: *(Slight pause, taking in.)* That's...that's true.

WOMAN: Of course it is.

A MOMENT OF WEAKNESS

(LAURA and WOMAN face out a moment, before…)

LAURA: *(Slight pause, then with difficulty.)* I guess I've always made it a point to be just that. To be…prepared, remain composed and…not allow myself to become overwhelmed if something unusual happened. I've lived what I've taught, basically. *(A weak grin…)* My husband calls me "The Rock" because…I've never panicked or…asked for advice, which is kind of funny being that he's a psychiatrist. That may explain why he sees one. *(Slight pause, with increased introspection.)* My father's always said that my mother and I are too much alike. Probably why we haven't spoken in… *(Slight pause.)* I don't know how prepared *she* was for this. All I know is that *I* sure wasn't.

(WOMAN takes LAURA's hand…)

WOMAN: She'll be fine, Laura. That's all you have to concern yourself with, okay? Now you have a nice flight coming up, so just try'n look forward to it.

LAURA: You're right.

WOMAN: There's no sense in letting yourself be consumed by ill feelings. Just enjoy your flight, you'll see your mother…and that'll be all she needs. And that'll be all *you* need. You both've butted heads long enough.

LAURA: *(Snickers weakly.)* Hm. I'm glad that I was fortunate enough to sit next to you.

WOMAN: Oh, stop. *I'm* glad. You're a dear.

LAURA: *(Humbly smiles.)* Tsch, what irony.

WOMAN: How's that?

LAURA: You're *my* motivational speaker.

WOMAN: Oh, no. No. As I said, it's just the truth, dear. It's simply the truth.

(WOMAN pats LAURA's hand before removing hers, as before. She looks out, as does LAURA.)

One more stop for me.

LAURA: Hm.

WOMAN: You don't have much farther to go either, huh?

LAURA: No, almost there.

(As they look at each other with affectionate grins, before LAURA takes hold of WOMAN's hand. They then turn out once again.)

(A moment, as WOMAN's grin gradually fades…)

WOMAN: Your flight's in less than an hour, you said?

LAURA: Mhm. The earliest one I could get.

WOMAN: *(Slight pause.)* You should reschedule.

LAURA: *(Unclear.)* What, Vera?

WOMAN: *(Turns to her, profoundly.)* You should reschedule your flight, dear.

LAURA: I'm…no, I don't think that'll be necessary, Vera. I'll make it. *(Looks at watch.)* I'll be fine.

WOMAN: Not if you're on that plane.

(WOMAN abruptly rises and looks out…)

LAURA: *(Slight pause, visibly chilled.)* What…? I'm… What…what are you saying?

WOMAN: *(As she looks out…)* You should reschedule your flight, dear.

(The STOP bell goes off!)

This is my stop.

LAURA: But…Vera, what…?

(WOMAN smiles weakly yet knowingly at LAURA…
before exiting off. Her departure is soon followed by
the sounds of the closing bus doors and the accelerating
engine.)

(All the while, LAURA looks off with obvious despair
and fear. She slowly turns to face out. She is now still for
the moment, before she urgently retrieves cell phone from
her purse, …dials…)

LAURA: *(Waits, then…)* Shit! *(Waits.)* Brian, it's…it's me. I'm still on the bus. I just… I don't know, I just had this very strange encounter with…with this older woman just now. She was…she was very comforting at first and then…she basically…tsch…she basically told me that I should reschedule my…my flight, as if she had this…sort of premonition about it, like…I dunno', like it was gonna' crash or something. She had these…these feelings about…things and I…I have to say, I kind of believe her. I just…I don't know what to think now. I don't know if she's just…nuts or… Just…give me a call as soon as you get this message, okay? I don't know what to do here. I don't…I don't know.

(She clicks off phone but holds it tightly within her
hands, …as the lights fade…)

DANIEL DAMIANO

End of Play

THE SURVEY

THE SURVEY

The Survey received its World Premiere as part of Studio Theater in Exile's Dramatist Theme Park in February 2025 in Peekskill, NY, with the following cast and director:

A SURVEY TAKER..........Basia Zak
A CITIZEN..................Joan Cavallo

Directed by Melanie Armer

Artistic Director: Mara Mills

Characters

A SURVEY TAKER – *Female, 30s-40s. Efficient, pleasant, enigmatic.*

A CITIZEN – *Female, 40s. Pleasant, intelligent, confident.*

A Pre-recorded Male Voice – *Generically formal.*

The Citizen's living room. The present.

A modest living room. The SURVEY TAKER, holding a tablet, and the CITIZEN sit across from each other. *The Survey Taker jots in her tablet after most of the Citizen's responses.

SURVEY TAKER: …and just to confirm, this is an anonymous survey.

CITIZEN: Understood.

SURVEY TAKER: And we also need to verify that you support us doing this survey with you and that, today, you consider yourself to be in a positive mindset, so as not to alter the results.

CITIZEN: Yes, I support it and, yes, I feel very good.

SURVEY TAKER: *(Jots…)* Wonderful. And we are ready to begin. *(A beat.)* Age?

CITIZEN: 44.

SURVEY TAKER: Gender?

CITIZEN: Well,…that should be clear, yes?

SURVEY TAKER: These days we find it best not to assume.

CITIZEN: *(A beat.)* Alright, female.

SURVEY TAKER: Thank you. Always?

CITIZEN: You mean, was I always…?

SURVEY TAKER: Yes.

CITIZEN: Yes.

SURVEY TAKER: Parents?

CITIZEN: *(A beat.)* Do I have them...?

SURVEY TAKER: Yes.

CITIZEN: Um, yes.

SURVEY TAKER: Very good.

CITIZEN: You have people who claim not to have parents?

SURVEY TAKER: I do.

CITIZEN: You mean, they were orphaned or invitro...?

SURVEY TAKER: I mean there are those who feel they've descended from an ostrich egg to an alien-operated space craft.

CITIZEN: Really?

SURVEY TAKER: We prefer not to judge. Merely assess.

CITIZEN: Well,...that seems fair.

SURVEY TAKER: This is a simple survey, remember.

CITIZEN: I see.

SURVEY TAKER: Living?

CITIZEN: Am I?

SURVEY TAKER: Your parents.

CITIZEN: Oh, sorry. I lost the thread there.

SURVEY TAKER: That's fine.

CITIZEN: No.

SURVEY TAKER: Causes?

CITIZEN: Of their…?

SURVEY TAKER: Yes.

CITIZEN: Cancer.

SURVEY TAKER: Father or mother?

CITIZEN: Both, I'm afraid.

SURVEY TAKER: (*A little too buoyant.*) So cancer and cancer.

CITIZEN: Um…yes.

SURVEY TAKER: Married?

CITIZEN: Myself? No.

SURVEY TAKER: Ever married?

CITIZEN: Yes.

SURVEY TAKER: How did the marriage conclude?

CITIZEN: Divorce.

SURVEY TAKER: Reason for the divorce?

CITIZEN: Um,…do I have to go into specifics?

SURVEY TAKER: It does help us to have a bit more detail, if you wouldn't mind.

CITIZEN: (*Slight pause.*) Okay. Well, he was a having an affair with another woman.

SURVEY TAKER: *(Slight pause.)* And?

CITIZEN: And...I didn't approve.

SURVEY TAKER: Ah. I see. Thank you.

CITIZEN: Does this...?

SURVEY TAKER: Children?

CITIZEN: Wha...? Uh, no.

SURVEY TAKER: Siblings?

CITIZEN: Two brothers and one sister.

SURVEY TAKER: Living?

CITIZEN: No.

SURVEY TAKER: Causes of death?

CITIZEN: Um, well, my brothers died of a heart attack and liver failure and my sister died of cancer.

SURVEY TAKER: *(A little too buoyant.)* So heart attack, liver failure, cancer.

CITIZEN: Um,...yes.

SURVEY TAKER: I see. Touch your nose with your right hand, please.

CITIZEN: My...?

SURVEY TAKER: Yes.

(The CITIZEN does so.)

SURVEY TAKER: Now touch your right ear with your left hand.

(The CITIZEN does so a bit more awkwardly.)

SURVEY TAKER: Thank you. *(Gazes out, with seriousness.)* A man is walking a dog on a quiet street in a quiet neighborhood on a quiet night. The dog sees something and pulls the man into the street where, much to the man's surprise, there is a steamroller approaching rapidly. The dog pulls the man toward the steamroller, which soon – *blanks* - the man. *(A beat, smiles.)* Please fill in the blank.

CITIZEN: Um, I... Kills?

(SURVEY TAKER looks at CITIZEN probingly for a moment, as the SURVEY TAKER remains awkwardly still.)

SURVEY TAKER: Kills.

CITIZEN: Yes, I... Was that not...?

SURVEY TAKER: *(Smiles.)* There's no right or wrong answer. Only *your* answer.

CITIZEN: Okay.

SURVEY TAKER: Again, this is a simple survey.

CITIZEN: *(Smiles.)* Right.

(SURVEY TAKER jots, stops.)

SURVEY TAKER: Profession?

CITIZEN: I was a lawyer.

SURVEY TAKER: How impressive.

THE SURVEY

CITIZEN: Well, thank you…

SURVEY TAKER: *(Over "you…")* But you're no longer a lawyer, you said.

CITIZEN: Uh, yes, correct.

SURVEY TAKER: Any current profession?

CITIZEN: I'm sort of in transition.

SURVEY TAKER: So you're not working.

CITIZEN: Well, I'm actually enjoying having time to myself, at the moment…

SURVEY TAKER: Blink once for me, please.

CITIZEN: Blink…?

SURVEY TAKER: Yes.

(CITIZEN does so.)

SURVEY TAKER: Honk twice for me, please.

CITIZEN: I… You said honk?

SURVEY TAKER: Yes, please.

CITIZEN: Um, alri… Honk? Honk?

SURVEY TAKER: *(Jots, then…)* Thank you. How are you maintaining an income?

CITIZEN: Well, right now, I have some savings, while figuring out my next...

SURVEY TAKER: Why did you conclude that the man must die?

CITIZEN: What man? Oh, are we back to the story...?

SURVEY TAKER: Yes.

CITIZEN: Well,...it just felt inevitable.

SURVEY TAKER: Inevitable, why?

CITIZEN: Well, I mean, it's a steamroller that he was being pulled into, yes?

SURVEY TAKER: Yes.

CITIZEN: Alright, so, I didn't really see another logical outcome.

SURVEY TAKER: I see.

(SURVEY TAKER looks at CITIZEN probingly for a moment, before brightly...)

SURVEY TAKER: Why did you decide to become a lawyer?

CITIZEN: Well, I guess because I wanted to help people.

SURVEY TAKER: And you stopped because...you no longer wanted to.

CITIZEN: Well, no, not that. I basically felt I no longer was able to help them effectively.

SURVEY TAKER: You were a bad lawyer.

CITIZEN: Uh, no. Actually, the opposite. I never lost a case.

THE SURVEY

SURVEY TAKER: Then why did you leave the profession?

CITIZEN: Well, honestly, I grew disheartened with how our legal system works in conjunction with society.

SURVEY TAKER: How, exactly?

CITIZEN: Well, in truth, I feel we have a system which basically prides itself on innocent until proven guilty, but our society too often belies that. And, frankly, it began to weigh on me a bit, so I decided...

SURVEY TAKER: *(Gazes out, with seriousness...)* A woman is driving along a quiet country road on a quiet day in a quiet town. She sees a car pulled over on the side of the road, and a large man is waving his hands in apparent need. The woman stops the car, the man aggressively comes to the passenger side, leans into the window and points a – *blank* - at her. *(A beat, smiles.)* Please fill in the blank.

CITIZEN: Um,...a gun?

> *(SURVEY TAKER looks at CITIZEN probingly for a moment...)*

SURVEY TAKER: A gun.

CITIZEN: Um,...yes?

> *(SURVEY TAKER jots, stops, then brightly...)*

SURVEY TAKER: Give me a specific example of why you are no longer working.

CITIZEN: You mean why I'm no longer a lawyer?

SURVEY TAKER: If that helps you.

CITIZEN: Um, okay, well... I represented someone who was perceived to have been guilty of...something. I believed that he wasn't. I believed that *he* believed that he wasn't...

SURVEY TAKER: But he was.

CITIZEN: No, he wasn't.

SURVEY TAKER: But he was found guilty.

CITIZEN: No, he was found *not* guilty.

SURVEY TAKER: And this was a reason why you left your profession?

CITIZEN: No, I left because the verdict didn't matter. You see?

SURVEY TAKER: No.

CITIZEN: Well, his reputation was tarnished.

SURVEY TAKER: But he was innocent, yes?

CITIZEN: But the perception outside the court ultimately ruled differently, you see?

SURVEY TAKER: No.

CITIZEN: In other words, the mere accusation that he was guilty was enough. I spent months tirelessly working to defend him and, in the end, it seemed he would've been better off being sentenced. You see?

SURIVEY TAKER: No.

CITIZEN: He became a social pariah based on *assumed* guilt.

SURVEY TAKER: And?

CITIZEN: He lost his job, his wife, his family, his house…

SURVEY TAKER: Did he commit suicide?

CITIZEN: Well, no…

SURVEY TAKER: Well, *that's* a good thing, yes?

CITIZEN: But he ended up having to move to another state.

SURVEY TAKER: Where he died in squalor?

CITIZEN: No, but…

SURVEY TAKER: Well, *that's* a good thing, yes?

CITIZEN: Well, not...

SURVEY TAKER: Could you stand up for me, please?

CITIZEN: I'm sorry?

SURVEY TAKER: Stand up for me. Please. This'll just take a second.

    (CITIZEN awkwardly does so.)

SURVEY TAKER: Raise your right hand.

    (CITIZEN does so.)

SURVEY TAKER: Cough once.

    (CITIZEN does so.)

Whistle twice.

CITIZEN: Whistle...?

SURVEY TAKER: Yes, please.

(CITIZEN does so, awkwardly.)

SURVEY TAKER: Thank you. Please sit.

(CITIZEN does so.)

CITIZEN: Is this intended to...?

SURVEY TAKER: Why did you elect to give the man a gun?

CITIZEN: What man?

SURVEY TAKER: The man with the car.

CITIZEN: Oh, the story.

SURVEY TAKER: Yes.

CITIZEN: Sorry, I'm not used to such fast transitions...

SURVEY TAKER: *(Over "transitions...")* You gave him a gun to point at the woman.

CITIZEN: Well, I, yes, I suppose I did but...

SURVEY TAKER: Yes?

CITIZEN: Well, I mean, you make it sound like I put him up to it.

SURVEY TAKER: I'm not saying that at all. I'm merely asking why you chose to arm him.

CITIZEN: Why? Well, what other option could one come to?

THE SURVEY

SURVEY TAKER: What do you mean, exactly?

CITIZEN: A strange, large man aggressively leans into the woman's passenger window, aims at her…?

SURVEY TAKER: I actually said *points*, not aims.

CITIZEN: Well, alright. Points, aims…

SURVEY TAKER: They are different.

CITIZEN: I know they're different, but look at your scenario.

SURVEY TAKER: What about it?

CITIZEN: Well, frankly, it's a bit leading.

SURVEY TAKER: Leading?

CITIZEN: It's a legal term. Yes. You coerced me into a reaction that I had no choice but to come up with. Just like the man crushed by a steamroller.

SURVEY TAKER: Well, in fairness, that wasn't the exact scenario.

CITIZEN: What do you mean?

SURVEY TAKER: Well, it was *you* who crushed him.

CITIZEN: Well, it was the likely conclusion, don't you think?

SURVEY TAKER: Not necessarily.

CITIZEN: He was being led into an oncoming steamroller by his idiotic dog.

SURVEY TAKER: But he didn't have to be crushed.

147

CITIZEN: Well, what else could he have been? Gently massaged?

SURVEY TAKER: Anything's possible.

CITIZEN: What, like a human baby emanating from an ostrich egg? Like being born from aliens?

SURVEY TAKER: Mam,...

CITIZEN: I'm sorry, but I was a lawyer. I dealt with sanity and insanity often. I know the difference.

SURVEY TAKER: I'm sure that you do...

CITIZEN: Well, I mean, I feel like you're alluding that my answers are abnormal somehow.

SURVEY TAKER: Mam,...

CITIZEN: I mean, is it wrong that the blanks that I filled in resulted in a man getting crushed to death and a woman possibly getting her head blown off?

SURVEY TAKER: You think she got her head blown off?

CITIZEN: Well, it's certainly possible.

SURVEY TAKER: How is it possible?

CITIZEN: He was "aggressive" and was aiming a gun at her.

SURVEY TAKER: Pointing not aiming.

CITIZEN: Alright, pointing, aiming. He clearly seemed to have ill intent, don't you think?

SURVEY TAKER: Well, only if he had a gun.

THE SURVEY

CITIZEN: He *did* have a gun!

SURVEY TAKER: But you gave it to him.

CITIZEN: Well, not because I… It just seemed…

SURVEY TAKER: Mam, there really is no need to panic about this. Again, this is a simple survey.

CITIZEN: I'm sorry, I've never done an in-person survey like this. It just seems a bit…

SURVEY TAKER: *(Gazes out, with seriousness…)* A woman is walking through a quiet park on a quiet night. She is alone. The silence is deafening. Soon she hears steps approaching her from behind. Instead of turning, she runs out of the park and into the street, except that a steamroller is quickly approaching and is obstructing her passage. The steps continue to approach her intensely from behind. She reaches into her purse, pulls out a gun, sharply looks back to find a young boy looking up at her. She *blanks* him. *(A beat, smiles.)* Please fill in the blank.

CITIZEN: *(Slight pause, carefully, then firmly.)* Um, I… She… Holds.

> *(SURVEY TAKER looks at CITIZEN probingly for a moment…)*

SURVEY TAKER: Holds.

CITIZEN: Yes.

SURVEY TAKER: *(Jots…)* You said you have no children?

CITIZEN: Correct.

SURVEY TAKER: Pets?

CITIZEN: Um, none currently.

SURVEY TAKER: But you've had them.

CITIZEN: In my life? Yes.

SURVEY TAKER: Causes of death?

CITIZEN: Of *their* deaths?

SURVEY TAKER: Yes.

CITIZEN: Well, it's not like we have the same DNA.

SURVEY TAKER: This isn't about genetics. Just your history.

CITIZEN: My God, I've had many.

SURVEY TAKER: That's fine. You don't have to note the type or breed, just the causes of their demise will be fine. From childhood, please.

CITIZEN: Jesus,... Alright, um. Well, from childhood; hit by a car, cancer, liver failure, kidney failure, cancer, liver failure...

SURVEY TAKER: I think that'll do. Is there anyone else?

CITIZEN: Anyone...?

SURVEY TAKER: Anyone who could take responsibility for you?

CITIZEN: For me? No.

SURVEY TAKER: And you reside here by yourself?

CITIZEN: Yes.

THE SURVEY

SURVEY TAKER: And you own or rent?

CITIZEN: Uh, well, I *did* own...

SURVEY TAKER: So now you rent.

CITIZEN: Well, I sold my house after the divorce, and thought I'd just...

SURVEY TAKER: So now you rent.

CITIZEN: Uh, yes, but...

SURVEY TAKER: Very good. So let's summarize thus far.

CITIZEN: Um, okay.

SURVEY TAKER: *(Briskly, referring to tablet...)* So you're a divorced middle-aged cuckquean and former lawyer who lives in a rental home alone with no offspring, 2 dead parents, 3 dead siblings, a bevvy of dead pets, and you're instinctive responses, based on the scenarios I provided, were that the man was crushed and the woman was quite possibly shot in the head.

CITIZEN: My God, *this* is what's going on my survey?

SURVEY TAKER: Well, this is why I'm here, after all.

CITIZEN: But what function does this kind of information serve?

SURVEY TAKER: Oh, a vital function. These sort of details help us gauge the mental and social stability of our country.

CITIZEN: Well, with all due respect, your summary of my life makes me sound like a walking plague.

SURVEY TAKER: How so?

CITIZEN: How...? It sounds like I'm this poor, lonely, bitter woman who wishes death on people.

SURVEY TAKER: Well, mam, we're not even finished.

CITIZEN: You know, I'm actually quite a centered, optimistic individual.

SURVEY TAKER: No one's disputing that...

CITIZEN: And quite accomplished, if I may say.

SURVEY TAKER: Mam,...

CITIZEN: I made twice what my ex-husband made. I put myself through law school...

SURVEY TAKER: Well, I did note that you are a *former* lawyer.

CITIZEN: Well, what about the boy?

SURVEY TAKER: The boy.

CITIZEN: Yes, the boy in your last scenario. I elected to *hold* him. Don't you remember? You should include that.

SURVEY TAKER: Ah, yes. Well, I wanted to address your response there.

CITIZEN: Address it how?

SURVEY TAKER: You elected to "hold" him, as you said, yes?

CITIZEN: Yes.

SURVEY TAKER: And yet you had a gun.

CITIZEN: Well, yes, but you gave me the gun in the scenario.

SURVEY TAKER: And yet you chose to disregard the gun.

CITIZEN: Well, not disregard it. I chose not to use it.

SURVEY TAKER: How can you choose not to use it?

CITIZEN: What do you mean how? It was a little boy.

SURVEY TAKER: Yes, it was.

CITIZEN: So why would I use the gun?

SURVEY TAKER: *(Suddenly intense...)* Because you hate children.

CITIZEN: What?!

SURVEY TAKER: Because you couldn't have them after your husband left you for another woman.

CITIZEN: What?!!!

SURVEY TAKER: *(Rises...)* You wanted to kill that boy and all that he represented, even more than you wanted to kill that man and woman. And yet you said you wanted to "hold" him, as if to suppress your homicidal instincts.

CITIZEN: Homicidal...?!

SURVEY TAKER: Admit it.

CITIZEN: Admit what?

SURVEY TAKER: You're a murderer!

CITIZEN: What?!

SURVEY TAKER: That's why you gave up the law, isn't it?! Because you wanted to *break* the law. Isn't that right?!

CITIZEN: No, it's not!!!

SURVEY TAKER: Guilty!

CITIZEN: What?

SURVEY TAKER: Guilty!!!

CITIZEN: Stop!

SURVEY TAKER: GUILTY!!!

CITIZEN: *(Rises...)* MY GOD, ARE YOU INSANE?!!! I DON'T WANNA KILL ANYONE!!! WHAT THE HELL KIND OF SURVEY IS THIS?

(The SURVEY TAKER gazes at the irate CITIZEN.)

SURVEY TAKER: *(Brightly, as she jots, as usual...)* Well, I think that about does it.

CITIZEN: I... Wait, I... What the hell is this?

SURVEY TAKER: You did quite well.

CITIZEN: Did what well? You come in here, ask me these bizarre questions, give me these strangely violent scenarios and then accuse me of being a murderer?

SURVEY TAKER: Mam, there's really no need for concern. Again, this is a simple survey...

CITIZEN: *(Over "a simple survey.")* A simple survey?!

154

SURVEY TAKER: Exactly. Oh, and you should receive a notification of your completion any second. If you can respond back, it'd be appreciated. Thank you so much for your participation.

(SURVEY TAKER opens door...)

Enjoy your evening.

(She exits. A moment.)

CITIZEN: My God,...

(We immediately hear an e-mail ding from the CITIZEN's nearby phone. She picks it up, pushes a prompt...)

A MAN'S VOICE: *"Thank you for participating in our survey. We have deemed your responses essential in contributing to the overall assessment regarding the mental status of our current society. To officially conclude your survey, we ask you to kindly complete this final scenario;*

SURVEY TAKER'S VOICE: *You're on a quiet road in a quiet town on a quiet night. You knock on a strange woman's door. She answers. You ask if she can participate in a brief survey. You ask her an odd assortment of questions, and she responds awkwardly but dutifully. She lives alone, is divorced, childless, petless, jobless and feels that society is prone to making abrupt judgements on those accused of wrong-doing. As a result, she feels she may be alone in her thinking and, perhaps,...alone in the world. **Or** perhaps she has become more enlightened by her experiences and, in those experiences, has become "optimistic" and "centered"*
        (A beat.)
You *feel she is - blank.*

(The CITIZEN contemplates this, clearly torn...)

CITIZEN: Well, I… *(Slight pause.)* I… *(Slight pause.)* I…

(She looks out, uncertain.)

(Lights out.)

End of Play

A LESSON IN
CAPTIVITY

A LESSON IN CAPTIVITY

A Lesson in Captivity received its World Premiere as part of the 2026 Downtown Urban Arts Festival in June 2026 at LaMama Experimental Theatre in New York City, with the following cast and director:

MS. COLÓN…....……..……..Judy Alvarez
LUKE…………....…………..…Sam Cruz
CASSIE…………..…………..Maya Patridge

Directed by Kathy Gail MacGowan

Artistic Director: Reg E. Gaines

*It received a previous Zoom presentation as part of fandango 4 Art House's Snippet Theatre Series in January 2021, with Judy Alvarez as Ms. Colon, Harry McMullen as Luke and Kat Warnusz-Steckel as Cassie.

Directed by Kathy Gail MacGowan

Cast of Characters

MS. COLÓN – *A teacher. 40s-50s. Spanish-American.*

LUKE – *A male student. 17. Caucasian.*

CASSIE – *A female student. 17. Caucasian.*

A classroom in a public high school, somewhere in the mid-or-southwestern United States.

Afternoon.

The Present.

(*Special Note – Ms. Colón's name is pronounced 'Kalone'. However, it should be noted that Luke intentionally mispronounces her name, hence the missing accent.)

Lights up on a classroom. MS. COLÓN sits behind desk, grading papers. LUKE, 17, and CASSIE, 17, sit at student desks, though they are at a considerable distance from each other.

CASSIE committedly does homework, while LUKE taps pen atop a blank piece of paper on his desk, obviously bored...

A moment.

LUKE: 'scuse me. Why do we have to do this?

MS. COLÓN: *(Slight pause, as she looks at him.)* Because you have to have something to do while you're here.

LUKE: It's not enough that we're here?

MS. COLÓN: No, it's not.

LUKE: Why? Broman let's us just chill.

MS. COLÓN: *(Slight pause.)* First of all, it's *Mr.* Broman, and it doesn't matter to me what you do or don't do when he's here.

LUKE: So we *have* to do this paper?

MS. COLÓN: Yes, Mr. Rawlings.

LUKE: Isn't that what, like, regular school is for?

MS. COLÓN: You're *in* school.

LUKE: No, I'm in detention. There's a difference.

MS. COLÓN: If you're in a classroom, then you're still in school. And if you're in school, you should have an assignment.

LUKE: Tsch...

MS. COLÓN: If you had homework, I'd allow you to do that, but you claim that you have none, correct?

LUKE: That's correct. I'm all caught up.

MS. COLÓN: Alright, then you can partake in this assignment that I gave you.

LUKE: Really?

MS. COLÓN: Yes. Really.

LUKE: *(Under breath...)* Jesus Christ...

MS. COLÓN: Mr. Rawlings.

LUKE: What?

MS. COLÓN: Please refrain from saying that.

LUKE: What, our lord and savior?

MS. COLÓN: That's enough.

LUKE: Why d'you automatically assume that I'm saying His name as a curse word?

MS. COLÓN: You weren't exactly saying it with reverence.

LUKE: I was jus' asking 'im for help.

MS. COLÓN: I think He has better things to do than get you out of writing an essay in detention.

LUKE: I jus' think it's funny. You jus' say the guy's name...

MS. COLÓN: I'm not gonna' repeat myself, Mr. Rawlings.

(CASSIE has sporadically observed this exchange, goes back to homework. MS. COLÓN soon after goes back to grading her papers.)

(After a moment, LUKE begins tapping his pen, as before,...)

MS. COLÓN: Mr. Rawlings,...

(LUKE looks at MS. COLÓN, before getting the hint. He looks back down at paper, clearly anxious and bored...)

LUKE: *(Under breath...)* God, it's like so much better when Broman's here.

MS. COLÓN: Well, I'm sorry to disappoint you. And, again, it's **Mr.** Broman.

LUKE: *(with "Mr. Broman")* **Mr.** Broman.

MS. COLÓN: Exactly.

LUKE: It's not like he's a teacher.

MS. COLÓN: Excuse me?

LUKE: He's a *gym* teacher. He's like one step away from janitor.

MS. COLÓN: Mr. Rawlings, I'm not about to debate Mr. Broman's profession with you. He's a teacher and he's also an elder. Do you understand?

LUKE: So?

MS. COLÓN: So you don't refer to adults by their last name alone.

LUKE: Tsch... God, when did detention become, like, this totalitarian society?

MS. COLÓN: That's a little extreme, wouldn't you say?

LUKE: No, I wouldn't. Seriously, it like went from restful to *1984*. I mean, what the hell?

MS. COLÓN: Restful?

LUKE: Yeah.

MS. COLÓN: This is detention, not a vacation.

LUKE: Feels a little worse than detention.

MS. COLÓN: Alright, Mr. Rawlings, just write your paper and be quiet, please. You only have 45 minutes. I'm sure you can endure.

> *(LUKE is tempted to respond, but resists, as CASSIE turns back to her homework. LUKE turns to Cassie, then back to MS. COLÓN, before half-assedly looking down at his blank paper. After a moment, he subconsciously starts to tap his pen again. After a moment, ...)*

MS. COLÓN: Mr. Rawlings.

> *(LUKE looks at her, stops. A moment.)*

> *(MS. COLÓN rises...)*

MS. COLÓN: I'll be right back. No talking.

LUKE: Yes, mam.

> *(MS. COLÓN exits.)*

(A moment, as LUKE looks over at CASSIE.)

LUKE: How come *you're* not doin' this? *(Slight pause.)* Huh?

CASSIE: What?

LUKE: How come you're not doin' this paper?

CASSIE: I obviously have homework.

LUKE: Oh, is it obvious?

CASSIE: I have an open calculus book right in front of me.

LUKE: Oh, well, look at you. So you get to avoid this hypothetical bullshit assignment. *"What could you've done to avoid being in detention today?"* Genius! Can't believe they fuckin' pay her.

> *(LUKE looks at CASSIE, who has turned her attention back to her homework.)*

LUKE: Seriously. I mean, who the fuck is she anyway? Some new sub?

CASSIE: I don't know.

LUKE: You ever see her?

CASSIE: No.

LUKE: It's like she jus' fell from the sky to fuck things up. Shit, lemme jus' sit. Confiscates our phones. It's bullshit, right? *(Slight pause.)* Right?

CASSIE: Please.

LUKE: Please what?

CASSIE: Just let me do my homework, okay? It's enough I'm even here.

LUKE: Tsch. But you sure are, ain't ya'?

(CASSIE continues to try and tune LUKE out, as she looks at her book...)

Yeah, why the hell *are* you here anyway? You're like Miss Goody-Good, right? Yeah, see your face all over. The bulletin board, yearbook. Runnin' for class president, runnin' for treasurer, runnin' for this'n that. Organizing all these funzy events. Shit, what happened?

CASSIE: None of your business.

LUKE: *(Rises...)* I'll bet I can guess.

CASSIE: Who cares?

LUKE: Hm, lemme see...

CASSIE: Who cares?! Just, please. Leave me alone.

(LUKE stares at her, trying to mask any embarrassment.)

LUKE: Tsch. Yeah, whatever.

(MS. COLÓN enters...)

MS. COLÓN: What's going on here?

LUKE: Nothin',

MS. COLÓN: Why are you standing?

LUKE: Jus' stretchin' my legs.

MS. COLÓN: Please sit.

LUKE: Mr. Broman let's us get up.

MS. COLÓN: I'm sure.

LUKE: Calisthenics. He's a gym teacher, remember?

MS. COLÓN: Sit down, Mr. Rawlings.

(LUKE eventually sits, before MS. COLÓN sits behind her desk. She goes back to grading her papers... A moment.)

LUKE: Are you new here or something?

MS. COLÓN: (Slight pause.) What exactly does it matter to you?

LUKE: What? Jus' curious. We haven't seen you around.

MS. COLÓN: (As she looks over her papers...) I arrived here last month.

LUKE: From?

MS. COLÓN: Mr. Rawlings, please.

LUKE: What? I'm just asking a question.

MS. COLÓN: This is not a social hour.

LUKE: I know.

MS. COLÓN: I gave you an assignment, so I want you focusing on that.

LUKE : But, Ms. Colon, what if I have a question?

MS. COLÓN: *(Slight pause.)* It's Co**lón**.

LUKE: What'd I say?

MS. COLÓN: You know what you said.

LUKE: I said it wrong? I thought…

MS. COLÓN: Do you have a question regarding the assignment or not?

LUKE: I do. No, sorry about the name. I thought I said it right…

MS. COLÓN: *(Over "said it right…")* What is the question?

LUKE: Yeah, well, uh…are you talking, like, in literal terms?

MS. COLÓN: What do you mean?

LUKE: You said it's gotta' be a paper on what we'd do differently. Is that literally or, like, metaphorically or biblically…?

MS. COLÓN: I think you know.

LUKE: No, I don't. That's why I'm asking you.

MS. COLÓN: What you could've done, literally, to alter your path from being here today.

LUKE: Hm.

MS. COLÓN: Alright?

LUKE: Kinda' moot, isn't it?

MS. COLÓN: I wouldn't say.

LUKE: To write about what you would've done differently if you already did what was done?

MS. COLÓN: I think you're misunderstanding the purpose of the assignment.

LUKE: And what's that?

MS. COLÓN: To learn from mistakes. To observe the results of your actions and think about what you could've done differently to alter an adverse outcome.

LUKE: But if the "adverse" outcome's already come, then what's the point?

MS. COLÓN: The point is that I see you've had similar outcomes before, Mr. Rawlings.

LUKE: So?

MS. COLÓN: So it stands to reason that you could benefit from this assignment. Maybe that'll give you a renewed perspective and, in so doing, you won't end up here again.

LUKE: You know why I'm here?

MS. COLÓN: Yes, I do.

LUKE: Well, it's all hearsay.

MS. COLÓN: Hearsay?

LUKE: I was falsely accused

MS. COLÓN: I know what hearsay means.

LUKE: Okay, so this paper has no relevance to me.

MS. COLÓN: I think it does, Mr. Rawlings.

LUKE: If I'm here 'cause a' something I didn't even do then what's the purpose a' writing about what I coulda' done differently?

MS. COLÓN: Well, if this was a first offense, I might give you the benefit of the doubt, but there appears to be a precedent.

LUKE: A what?

MS. COLÓN: You've done similar things before.

LUKE: How do you know? You weren't there.

CASSIE: *(Under breath...)* Please.

LUKE: What was that?

CASSIE: Why don' you just write the paper?

LUKE: Why don't *you*?

CASSIE: I have homework.

LUKE: *(Rises...)* Good for you. Then mind your own business.

MS. COLÓN: *(Over "business...")* That's enough! Mr. Rawlings, sit down. Ms. Yates, finish your homework, please.

(LUKE and CASSIE continue to glare at each other.)

MS. COLÓN: Mr. Rawlings.

(After a moment, LUKE sits.)

169

(A moment.)

LUKE: Can I use the bathroom?

(MS. COLÓN looks at him skeptically.)

What? I really gotta' go. I had like three Sprites.

MR. COLÓN: *(Slight pause.)* Go. Five minutes.

(LUKE exits.)

CASSIE: He is such a freak.

MS. COLÓN: That's not necessary.

CASSIE: No, I'm sorry, Ms. Colón, but he is. And I know what he did.

MS. COLÓN: *(Indifferent, as she grades...)* Oh?

CASSIE: I have a friend in the same English class. She saw everything, so he's totally lying. Why he even keeps going to school is, like, a mystery.

MS. COLÓN: Well, I'd like to think there's hope for every-body.

CASSIE: Oh, my God, Ms. Colón, if you'd been here long enough, you'd know that just about every teacher's given up on him.

MS. COLÓN: *(Looks at Cassie.)* And how would you know that?

CASSIE: 'cause I know different people who have classes with him. He pretty much just sleeps and the teachers let 'im because they'd rather he be unconscious. He doesn't get anything from this place. You think he ever actually does homework? My God, if you looked at his notebook, probably all you'd find is drawings of demons and swastikas. God knows what's in his locker. He's probably got, like, dead rabbits in there or something. And then he actually tries to ask girls out. I mean,... Whatever. I'm just saying.

MS. COLÓN: Well, I think you've said enough, Ms. Yates.

CASSIE: *(Slight pause.)* Sorry.

MS. COLÓN: Just finish your homework, alright?

(CASSIE goes back to her homework, somewhat embarrassed. LUKE enters.)

(He sits at his desk.)

MS. COLÓN: Were you smoking?

LUKE: *(Slight pause.)* Who, me?

MS. COLÓN: I smell smoke.

LUKE: Oh my God, we better evacuate! *(...rises...)*

MS. COLÓN: Sit down, Mr. Rawlings. You know what I'm referring to.

LUKE: *(As he sits...)* The bathroom already smelled of it. It musta' just rubbed off.

MS. COLÓN: *(Slight pause.)* Alright, Mr. Rawlings, I think we've had enough events and we don't have much time left, so why don't you do some writing.

LUKE: My false confession?

MS. COLÓN: If that's how you'd like to refer to it.

LUKE: I would indeed.

MS. COLÓN: Well, then why don't you just indulge me, okay?

LUKE: Why should I?

MS. COLÓN: *(A beat.)* Because I asked you to.

LUKE: And I can say no.

MS. COLÓN: Well, now I'm not asking.

LUKE: And I can still say no. This is a free country last time I checked.

MS. COLÓN: *(Slight pause.)* Mr. Rawlings, why do I get the sneaking suspicion that you actually like it here.

LUKE: Like it here?

MS. COLÓN: Well, it seems that you enjoy a certain…way of acting. You have a certain persona, and maybe this is the only way that persona can function.

LUKE: That's funny.

MS. COLÓN: Is it?

LUKE: Or maybe you're just used to dutiful little angels, like this one, who make it easy for ya'.

CASSIE: *(Under breath…)* Unbelievable.

LUKE: Shut up!

CASSIE: You shut up! God!

MS. COLÓN: *(Over "God!")* That's enough! Both of you!

LUKE: No, seriously, though...

MS. COLÓN: I'm serious too, Mr. Rawlings.

LUKE: *(Over "Mr. Rawlings...")* Nah, but hear me out. I mean, you come over here, new job or whatever. You get to make money to watch a coupla' kids in detention. And if I wasn't here, you could just do whatever you want.

MS. COLÓN: And what do you assume that would be?

LUKE: I dunno'. Whatever.

MS. COLÓN: So I'm not understanding your point, Mr. Rawlings. Are you protesting writing this paper because you think it's unjust or because you think I don't deserve to earn a living unless I deal with a problematic individual?

LUKE / CASSIE: I'm not problematic. / That's the understatement of the year.

LUKE: *(To Cassie.)* Shut up!

MS. COLÓN: Mr. Rawlings, that's enough.

LUKE: *(To Ms. Colón.)* I'm a problem 'cause I don't wana' write some BS paper?

MS. COLÓN: That's quite enough.

LUKE: *(Rises...)* Yeah, and I *do* protest. I'm innocent, dude!

MS. COLÓN: I'm not a "dude", Mr. Rawlings.

LUKE: Yeah, okay.

MS. COLÓN: No, not *"yeah, okay"*. And if you had any sincere interest in representing yourself as "innocent", I'd think you'd have a little more respect for someone who didn't even put you here, Mr. Rawlings.

LUKE: You're all part of the same machine.

MS. COLÓN: You think so?

LUKE: Yeah, I do. And y'know what? Detention *was* the best parta' this place 'cause at least *Mr.* Broman jus' left us alone.

MS. COLÓN; I see. He did what he wanted and let you do what you want.

LUKE: Pretty much.

MS. COLÓN: And so you don't have a problem with *Mr. Broman* getting paid for that.

LUKE: Hey, he can take money for sittin' on his ass, as long as he doesn't bust mine.

MS. COLÓN: Ah, I see. Sit down, Mr. Rawlings.

LUKE: *(Over "Mr. Rawlings...")* But you got an axe to grind.

MS. COLÓN: *(Slight pause.)* An axe to grind.

LUKE: *(With a smile.)* Yeah.

CASSIE: *(Rises...)* Do you want me to get Mr. Kimble, Ms. Colón?

MS. COLÓN: *(Rises...)* Ms. Yates, it's fine. Please sit.

LUKE: Yeah, she doesn't need your help.

CASSIE: Oh my God, don't even talk to me!

LUKE: Don't butt into my conversation.

MS. COLÓN: *(Over "conversation")* Mr. Rawlings, sit down right now!

LUKE: No, I don't need friggin' Snow White chimin' in. It's none a' her business…

CASSIE / MS. COLÓN: *(Over "business")*
Shut up! / Mr. Rawlings, I am losing my patience with you!

LUKE: *(to Cassie, over "losing my patience…")* All she gives a crap about is gettin' brownie points.

CASSIE: *(Over "brownie points…")* Shut the hell up!

> *(MS. COLÓN comes from behind her desk as LUKE approaches CASSIE…)*

LUKE: Lota good it did ya', right? 'cause here you are with me.

MS. COLÓN / CASSIE: *(Over "with me")*
Mr. Rawlings,… / One time!

LUKE: Still here.

CASSIE: One time! You *live* here!

LUKE: *(Over "You live here!")* Still here, Ms. Yates! In detention.

MS. COLÓN: Mr. Rawlings, go back to your desk and sit down…

LUKE: *(Over "back to your desk...")* Not at your precious corner of the cafeteria eatin' finger sandwiches with your bulimic snob girlfriends...

MS. COLÓN: *(Over "snob girlfriends...")* Mr. Rawlings, I'm not going to say this again...!

LUKE: *(Over "say this again...")* Detention's a great equalizer, ain't it?

CASSIE: *(Sobbing, over "ain't it")* You're a fucking miscreant!!!

MS. COLÓN: *(Over "miscreant")* SIT DOWN, MR. RAWLINGS, OR I'LL TAKE YOU DOWN TO MR. KIMBLE'S OFFICE RIGHT NOW. DO YOU UNDERSTAND?!

(A moment, as LUKE looks at CASSIE crying into her hands, somewhat victoriously.)

Now, Mr. Rawlings.

(He looks back at MS. COLÓN, then slowly makes his way back to his desk on the other side of the room.)

(After a moment, MS. COLÓN approaches CASSIE's desk. They speak out of earshot of Luke.)

MS. COLÓN: Are you okay?

CASSIE: *(Wiping her eyes...)* He is such a freak. I hate him.

MS. COLÓN: Alright, just calm down...

CASSIE: *(Over "calm down...")* Why do I even have to be in the same room with him? I peek at a few stupid answers on a test, and I'm quarantined with Jeffrey Dahmer.

MS. COLÓN: Ms. Yates, please,...

CASSIE: *(In a lower tone...)* I heard he makes ashtrays out of cat skulls.

MS. COLÓN: I doubt that's true.

CASSIE: Why? You think he's above it? Students shouldn't be forced to be around him. All he does is pick on people and smoke cigarettes. He's a like a walking plague.

MS. COLÓN: Why don't you go to the ladies room and wash your face. Take a few minutes. We don't have much more time.

CASSIE: I shouldn't even be here.

MS. COLÓN: *(A beat.)* Well, apparently you should.

CASSIE: No, I shouldn't, Ms. Colón. I'm a good student who just made a mistake.

MS. COLÓN: And I guess that's why you're here.

CASSIE: I'm acing everything. It's just this Calculus test, and my mother... She's...

MS. COLÓN: *(Slight pause.)* She told you to cheat?

CASSIE: No, she... Anyway.

MS. COLÓN: *(Slight pause.)* Ms. Yates, just relax and go to the restroom, alright? Take a few minutes.

> *(CASSIE looks over at LUKE, who has had his head down, before exiting. He sits up upon the door closing.)*

> *(MS. COLÓN observes him, before heading back to*

her desk.)

LUKE: She's a pieca' work, huh?

(MS. COLÓN looks at him.)

LUKE: Don't let 'er fool ya'. She only cried 'cause she knows what she is now. No one talks to her like that. She's gotta' end up in here to get a dose of reality.

MS. COLÓN: I don't think you should be taking any sort of credit.

LUKE: Hell, *I* do.

MS. COLÓN: Think again.

LUKE: See that's the thing. I *should* be getting credit. My grade point average should actually go up for what I can do to phonies like her. This school doesn't have a clue. It rewards people like her.

MS. COLÓN: And yet she's here like you, Mr. Rawlings.

LUKE: Yeah, but her type's never in detention, and she probably does all kinds a' sordid crap, but she gets away with it because she organizes bake-offs'n stuff.

MS. COLÓN: She's a good student who made an error in judgement.

LUKE: Oh, yeah. That's right. She made an "error in judgement" and I'm a delinquent, right?

MS. COLÓN: I didn't say that…

LUKE: Yeah, sure, she's gonna' be a doctor or a lawyer or a politician, and I'm the one who everyone thinks is gonna' be stockin' groceries until I'm 90 with my teeth fallin' on the floor.

MS. COLÓN: Mr. Rawlings...

LUKE: And then some little kids'll pick 'em up and think it's, like, corn or somethin' and their parents'll say, *"Don't touch that! He doesn't have much but at least let 'im have his rotting teeth!"*

(LUKE laughs, observed awkwardly by MS. COLÓN...)

MS. COLÓN: Is that how you see yourself?

LUKE: Hell, no. It's what *she* thinks. She thought she was a million miles away from me, and look at her now.

(CASSIE enters, sits. A moment.)

MS. COLÓN: Are you okay?

CASSIE: Fine.

LUKE: Yeah, she's fine.

CASSIE: Don't speak for me.

MS. COLÓN: Ms. Yates, please...

CASSIE: *(Rises, over "please...")* No, I don't want him to speak for me or to me or even look at me.

LUKE: Whatever, prom queen.

MS. COLÓN: Mr. Rawlings, enough. Ms. Yates, we're almost through here, alright? Just sit down and resume your work. Mr. Rawlings, you can put your head down.

(...as CASSIE sits...)

LUKE: But I'm almost finished with my paper.

MS. COLÓN: I'm sure.

LUKE: I'm serious. It's all up here. I can give, like, an oral presentation. See, I've been ruminating about it and, like, formulating it as an oral essay. It's almost done. Can I recite what I got?

MS. COLÓN: No.

LUKE: Why not?

MS. COLÓN: I said no.

LUKE: You inspired me.

MS. COLÓN: Mr. Rawlings,…

LUKE: It's your own assignment. Jesus Christ!

MS. COLÓN: *(Rises...)* Mr. Rawlings, I told you once.

LUKE: What, about the Jesus thing?

MS. COLÓN: You have two more detentions.

CASSIE: *(Under her breath...)* It's not enough.

LUKE: Mind your own business, Molly Ringworm…!

MS. COLÓN: *(Over "Molly...")* Mr. Rawlings, be quiet. Ms. Yates, I don't need your help here.

LUKE: Yeah, Miss Priss. Ms. **Colon**'s got me totally under control.

CASSIE: You are such a disrespectful piece of shit...

MS. COLÓN: *(Over "piece of...")* That's enough! Mr. Rawlings, if I see you so much as look in Ms. Yates' direction, say the lord's name in vain or say my name like it's a part of the anatomy again, I'm bringing you down to Mr. Kimble's office, do you understand?

LUKE: Heck, jus' bring me down now. What do I care?

MS. COLÓN: *(A beat.)* I really don't think you want that, Mr. Rawlings.

LUKE: Hey, you're clearly trying to prove that you can, like, handle me and you can't, so why waste time? Bring me down. He don't expect much from me, but...he may be disappointed in *you*. Right?

(A moment, as MS. COLÓN glares at LUKE.)

MS. COLÓN: You know, Mr. Rawlings, I don't know you from Adam outside of what I've observed today, but what I *have* observed is someone who really is misusing the opportunity that you have at this school.

LUKE: Oh, yeah? And what opportunity is that?

MS. COLÓN: *(A beat.)* The opportunity to not become a criminal.

LUKE: *(Chuckles...)* You know what I think?

MS. COLÓN: Mr. Rawlings, I think we're done...

LUKE: *(Over "we're done...".)* I think you got an issue with white men.

(MS. COLÓN looks intensely at LUKE...)

181

CASSIE: Oh, my God.

LUKE: Yeah. See, I'm a white guy and you wana', like, suppress me. Kimble's a white dude and you don't wana' act like you need his help 'cause you wana', like, prove somethin'. Right? But I'm the one who's in detention, so you think you can, like, pay the white man back, right? Treat me like you think White America's treated your people.

MS. COLÓN / CASSIE: My people? / Oh, my God...

LUKE: *(Rises...)* No, hear me out. You look at me and probably see your kids or nieces or nephews wrapped in foil on the floor of some detention center, so you wana' impart your vengeance on me, right?

CASSIE: You should be so ashamed of yourself, Luke...

LUKE: *(Over "yourself...")* Oh, don't you even start. Your whole life's a joke!

MS. COLÓN: *(Over "a joke...")* MR. RAWLINGS! *(Slight pause, with restraint.)* I want you to go to Mr. Kimble's office right now.

LUKE: *(Rises victoriously, with hands in the air...)* Victory is mine, said the Lord!

MS. COLÓN: Yes, that's right. You're the victor.

LUKE: Hah! See?

MS. COLÓN: Please leave.

LUKE: See?

MS. COLÓN: Right now.

LUKE: See?

MS. COLÓN: Right now, Mr. Rawlings. There's nothing else keeping you here. Just take your victory lap down to the principal's office.

LUKE: What, you're gonna' trust me to go down by myself?

MS. COLÓN: *(Slight pause.)* No, believe it or not, I *don't* trust you. Not in the slightest.

LUKE: *(A beat.)* Oooo-kay, so…

MS. COLÓN: So go to his office, Mr. Rawlings,…or continue walking until you're past his office, out of the school, all the way home and, eventually, to juvenile detention, then to jail, then to prison…and then to an almost certain and horrible death. Whatever option you choose, I think the end result will pretty much be the same,…because I'll tell you what probably nobody else will care enough to say to you in your lifetime; you're a Goddamned menace. And you should be so lucky to live to be a 90 year-old toothless grocer.

> *(MS. COLÓN and LUKE's eyes remain intensely locked,*
> *though the intensity of MS. COLÓN's gaze appears to*
> *trump LUKE's, as CASSIE nervously looks on.*
> *Eventually, LUKE awkwardly motions to door…)*

Wait.

> *(He stops, as MS. COLÓN pulls his cell phone out from*
> *her desk drawer and slams it onto to her desk.)*

Take your phone before I smash it to pieces.

> *(He looks at her, almost stunned at her threat. He goes to*
> *her desk, looks at her…, then sharply takes phone, before*
> *eventually…slamming the door on his way out.)*

(MS. COLÓN continues to gaze at the door, as CASSIE looks at her. A moment.)

CASSIE: Oh, my God. Are you okay?

MS. COLÓN: *(Slight pause.)* I'm fine. *(Looks at clock.)* Why don't you start packing up, Ms. Yates. I'll let you go a few minutes early.

CASSIE: *(Slight pause.)* Thank you.

(MS. COLÓN sits, attempting to decompress, as CASSIE gathers her books into her bag-pack, before gingerly turning to her...)

I don't think anyone's put him in his place like that. That was, like, really impressive, Ms. Colón.

(MS. COLÓN tepidly nods, as she looks at her papers before her...)

(CASSIE moves towards the door, before turning back to MS. COLÓN, awkwardly but dutifully.)

I know I needed to be here, Ms. Colón. It's just... A lot's expected of me, and sometimes it's... Well,... Anyway, I know it was wrong.

MS. COLÓN: So maybe he *does* serve a purpose, after all.

CASSIE: *(A beat.)* Whata' ya' mean?

MS. COLÓN: Maybe if you have any temptations to cheat in the future, you'll recall today...and think better.

CASSIE: *(Slight pause.)* No, that's not what I... He's just a... He's not even worth... I'm not gonna' give him credit for...

(MS. COLÓN looks at CASSIE, knowingly, while CASSIE has a hard time returning the look, becoming almost embarrassed at how exposed she now feels. She starts to exit...)

Oh. Um...my phone.

(She approaches MS. COLÓN, who removes CASSIE's phone from her desk, hands it to her.)

Thanks.

(CASSIE goes to door, stops, awkwardly...)

Bye.

MS. COLÓN: *(Slight pause.)* Goodbye, Ms. Yates.

(CASSIE exits.)

(MS. COLÓN continues to gaze at door, then faces out, still shaken by the events that have transpired.)

(Lights fade.)

End of Play

THE
ENLIGHTENMENT OF
MRS. CARTWELL

THE ENLIGHTENMENT OF MRS. CARTWELL

The Enlightenment of Mrs. Cartwell received its NYC Premier as part of the 2009 Estrogenius Festival at Manhattan Theatre Source, with the following cast and director:

MRS. CARTWELL...........Mia Moreland
MRS. WHOLEWIG..........Laura Piquado
MRS. LUVADORE......Annalisa Loeffler
MRS. PEACOCK......Anna Emily Altman

Directed by Kathy Gail MacGowan

Co-Executive Producers: Fiona Jones and Jen Thatcher

The Enlightenment of Mrs. Cartwell received its World Premiere in 2009 at the Old Opera House Theatre Company in Charleston, West Virginia, where it also was the recipient of the Silver Stage Award.

Cast of Characters

MRS. CARTWELL - *A refined Englishwoman, late 30's-40's. Only slightly larger than the others.*

MRS. WHOLEWIG - *A refined Englishwoman, late 30's-40's.*

MRS. LUVADORE - *A refined Englishwoman, mid-to-late 30's. The most glamorous.*

MRS. PEACOCK - *A refined Englishwoman, late 30's-40's.*

A café' near Hyde Park in London, late 18ᵗʰ Century.

THE ENLIGHTENMENT OF MRS. CARTWELL

MRS. WHOLEWIG and MRS. CARTWELL, standing. A tall potted plant is nearby, more or less center.

MRS. WHOLEWIG: Are you certain?

MRS. CARTWELL: I distinctly heard her.

MRS. WHOLEWIG: How ghastly.

MRS. CARTWELL: She spewed her whispered wisecrackery with the venom of a python.

MRS. WHOLEWIG: I must say that I'm rather stunned.

MRS. CARTWELL: Stunned because you've never heard her say something so obscene?

MRS. WHOLEWIG: Well, only regarding women for whom we all share a similar distaste,…

MRS. CARTWELL: Yes, well, it appears that Mrs. Luvadore's boundaries have eroded.

MRS. WHOLEWIG: …and certainly not within hearing range.

MRS. CARTWELL: Yes, well, little did she know that this time she chose a victim with hypersensitive ears.

MRS. WHOLEWIG: Well, I suppose it's possible.

MRS. CARTWELL: Of course, it is. I bloody heard it.

MRS. WHOLEWIG: But we've always reserved our judgements towards those *outside* of our social circle.

MRS. CARTWELL: I'm aware.

MRS. WHOLEWIG: It's difficult to fathom how one such as herself, with whom we share an acquaintanceship, would violate our unspoken code of ethics.

MRS. CARTWELL: Truly.

MRS. WHOLEWIG: And yet...

MRS. CARTWELL: Indeed.

MRS. WHOLEWIG: Are you certain there is not the remotest possibility that you somehow misinterpreted...?

MRS. CARTWELL: My dear, when one feels offense, there is no misinterpretation. I distinctly heard her murmur to Mrs. Peacock as I walked away yesterday. I was right in this very spot, unbeknownst to her. And if you were in attendance, you would've borne witness.

MRS. WHOLEWIG: Or perhaps she would've refrained completely, as she is certainly aware that we are...

MRS. CARTWELL: Yes.

MRS. WHOLEWIG: Indeed.

MRS. CARTWELL: Of course.

MRS. WHOLEWIG: Did you say anything to her?

MRS CARTWELL: Words failed me. I was aghast.

MRS. WHOLEWIG: Yes, I would imagine.

MRS. CARTWELL: I went from apoplectic white to angered crimson within minutes before storming away. I'd never been so humiliated.

MRS. WHOLEWIG: Well, my dear, the best thing to do was react in the ladylike manner in which you did.

MRS. CARTWELL: *(Bitterly.)* Hm.

MRS. WHOLEWIG: *(A beat.)* What?

MRS. CARTWELL: As I lay awake last night, that very phrase haunted me; "Ladylike". How ladies of our stature resolve issues such as these; walk away, remain silent. Or, at best, exclaim *"Well, I never"* and then cower under a tree like a dejected squirrel.

MRS. WHOLEWIG: No one is telling you to cower, my dear.

MRS. CARTWELL: Then act as if it was never said?

MRS. WHOLEWIG: Well, yes.

MRS. CARTWELL: And yet know for a fact that it was. That this seeming acquaintance of ours has this opinion of me?

MRS. WHOLEWIG: My dear…

MRS. CARTWELL: Absolutely not. I won't sleep another night if I contain myself.

MRS. WHOLEWIG: What on earth are you proposing?

MRS. CARTWELL: Well, I'm…I'm proposing to demand an apology,…or else!

MRS. WHOLEWIG: Or else?!

MRS. CARTWELL: Indeed.

MRS. WHOLEWIG: Well, that sounds so egregiously masculine. Or else what?!

MRS. CARTWELL: Or else... Well, I'm not certain. What other options does a woman have?

MRS. WHOLEWIG: Why, none, of course. My dear, you really do need to gather yourself.

MRS. CARTWELL: Gather myself? My dear, I assure you that if it was **your** rump she declared as "ample", you'd be as indignant as myself.

MRS. WHOLEWIG: Well, even if she *did* say it, perhaps it wasn't intended as an insult.

MRS. CARTWELL: A lady you have thus far perceived as a friendly acquaintance and co-conspirator in gossip proclaims in a hushed tone that your bottom is the equivalent of a horse carriage, and I'm not to find that utterly humiliating?

MRS. WHOLEWIG: She didn't say *that*.

MRS. CARTWELL: She may as well have.

MRS. WHOLEWIG: Well,...perhaps it is only really humiliating to the envious proclaimer.

MRS. CARTWELL: *(Slight pause.)* What are you saying?

MRS. WHOLEWIG: Well,...as we know, Mrs. Luvadore has always possessed a certain grandiloquence, which may very well be a compensation for certain deficiencies in her character.

MRS. CARTWELL: You're saying that she's jealous?

MRS. WHOLEWIG: Well,...perhaps.

MRS. CARTWELL: Really?

MRS. WHOLEWIG: It's certainly possible.

MRS. CARTWELL: Well, that would certainly be nice.

MRS. WHOLEWIG: Why, she's rather thin, yes?

MRS. CARTWELL: Why, yes.

MRS. WHOLEWIG: Almost malnourished, if you will.

MRS. CARTWELL: Yes.

MRS. WHOLEWIG: Why, she hardly even *has* a rump.

MRS. CARTWELL: Not that I can find.

MRS. WHOLEWIG: Very little meat on her bones, which may very well stem from a low sense of self-worth.

MRS. CARTWELL: Why is that?

MRS. WHOLEWIG: Well, she may not be happily married.

MRS. CARTWELL: Really.

MRS. WHOLEWIG: Rumor has it.

MRS. CARTWELL: Does it?

MRS. WHOLEWIG: Well, no, but…anything's possible, yes?

MRS. CARTWELL: Why, yes.

MRS. WHOLEWIG: Her husband is often on safari, leaving her often alone.

MRS. CARTWELL: Yes.

MRS. WHOLEWIG: How content can a woman be, under those circumstances?

MRS. CARTWELL: I'd imagine not very at all.

MRS. WHOLEWIG: There, you see?

MRS. CARTWELL: *(Elated.)* I do.

MRS. WHOLEWIG: Now you have perspective, my dear. All of your indignance was for not. Now shall we..?

MRS. CARTWELL: *(Suddenly pensive.)* And yet still.

MRS. WHOLEWIG: Still?

MRS. CARTWELL: I feel at the very least I should address this issue with Mrs. Luvadore.

MRS. WHOLEWIG: But, my dear, what is there to address?

MRS. CARTWELL: I need to believe that her comment was in fact out of envy and not malice.

MRS. WHOLEWIG: But I thought we agreed…

MRS. CARTWELL: Yes, but what you and I agree upon may not pertain to her thinking. If her intent *was* to humiliate me, then perhaps all I am to her is a pig in a petticoat? Then all I can think is that there's no limit to what *she* can think, or say behind my back, or to what she may've already said to whomever about myself and my…my…

MRS. WHOLEWIG: Oh, really now…

MRS. CARTWELL: Well, at the very least, I can ask her intent.

MRS. WHOLEWIG: And then what if she takes offense? Has that occurred to you?

MRS. CARTWELL: Well,…

MRS. WHOLEWIG: Perhaps your accusation may, in fact, embarrass *her*, thus exploiting her jealousy, thus leading to her resentment. And then what would that bode for your reputation?

MRS. CARTWELL: My reputation?

MRS. WHOLEWIG: Well, Mrs. Luvadore has proven herself most adept at stirring gossip, certainly more expeditiously than the rest of us.

MRS. CARTWELL: Something *we've* often been jealous of.

MRS. WHOLEWIG: Indeed. Therefore, what will it mean if word got out that you accused her falsely.

MRS. CARTWELL: I see.

MRS. WHOLEWIG: A paranoid woman is never in fashion, my dear.

MRS. CARTWELL: Perhaps you're right.

MRS. WHOLEWIG: I believe I am.

MRS. CARTWELL: Well,…alright.

MRS. WHOLEWIG: Very well. Now, there is Mrs. Luvadore and Mrs. Peacock at our usual table. Simply act as if it was never said, and be all the more refined.

(...*as a light appears on MRS. LUVADORE & MRS. PEA COCK, seated. They laugh amongst themselves, before CARTWELL yanks WHOLEWIG back.*)

MRS. CARTWELL: Wait.

MRS. WHOLEWIG: Oh, dear…

MRS. CARTWELL: Let me first attempt to gather the source of their amusement.

MRS. WHOLEWIG: Oh, my dear, really...

MRS. CARTWELL: Please, indulge me in this regard. I haven't asked much of you, have I?

MRS. WHOLEWIG: *(Begrudgingly...)* Well, alright.

(They crouch behind the nearby plant.)

MRS. LUVADORE: Oh, my dear, Mrs. Peacock, in all candor, I can't recall ever seeing anything quite so enormous.

MRS. PEACOCK: How very frightening.

MRS. LUVADORE: Well, at first, certainly. After all, you simply do not know what one that large is capable of.

MRS. PEACOCK: One can only imagine.

MRS. LUVADORE: It could've been rather explosive, depending on whether she'd recently eaten or not. Especially being in such a close proximity.

MRS. CARTWELL: *(Sotto voce...)* Oh, my dear Lord. They **are** talking about me.

MRS. LUVADORE: However, one must be courteous to all God's creatures, even in their rather ample and grotesque forms.

MRS. CARTWELL: She's speaking about me as if I were some hideous carnival freak.

MRS. LUVADORE: Though it really is all a matter of physical positioning. As someone once told me, you are always safest in front of one's eyes as opposed to behind one's rear.

THE ENLIGHTENMENT OF MRS. CARTWELL

*(Mrs. Luvadore and Mrs. Peacock share a laugh,
before Mrs. Cartwell bursts on...)*

Oh, well, hello, Mrs. Cartwell. Mrs. Wholewig.

MRS. WHOLEWIG: Mrs. Luvadore. Mrs. Peacock.

MRS. PEACOCK: Mrs. Wholewig. Mrs. Cartwell.

MRS. CARTWELL: I will dispense with my usual courtesies,
if I may be so bold.

MRS. WHOLEWIG: My dear...

MRS. CARTWELL: In lieu of kindly requesting that you STOP
CARRYING ON ABOUT MY BLOODY BUM!!!

MRS. LUVADORE / MRS. PEACOCK
What?!! / Oh, my word...

MRS. WHOLEWIG: My dear, please...

MRS. LUVADORE: Mrs. Cartwell, I'm afraid I'm at a bit of a
loss as to what you're insinuating.

MRS. CARTWELL: I just overheard you divulging about the
enormity of my "enormous"...you know.

MRS. LUVADORE: What?

MRS. CARTWELL: You know very well.

MRS. WHOLEWIG: My dear...

MRS. CARTWELL: My seat!

LUVADORE & PEACOCK: Your seat?!

MRS. CARTWELL: Yes, my seat. And don't defend her, Mrs. Peacock. You are equally responsible.

MRS. PEACOCK: Well, I...

MRS. LUVADORE: My dear, I'm afraid that you're sadly mistaken.

MRS. CARTWELL: Oh, am I.

MRS. LUVADORE: I'm afraid so.

MRS. CARTWELL: How dare you. And to think that I came here with the intent of letting your callous comment yesterday slip through my ears, only to find you revisiting your maliciousness behind my back, **and yet right under my nose**!

MRS. LUVADORE: Mrs. Cartwell,...

MRS. CARTWELL: I've always tolerated your arrogance, so long as it was directed outside of our circle, but you have emphatically crossed the line with me, madam. At the very least, I want an apology. And if you resist, then...then...!!!

MRS. LUVADORE: Then what?

MRS. CARTWELL: I...I...I hereby challenge you ...**to a duel!**

LUVADORE, PEACOCK & WHOLEWIG: A DUEL?!!!

MRS. LUVADORE: For what I just said?!

MRS. CARTWELL: And for yesterday?

MRS. LUVADORE: What did I say yesterday?

MRS. CARTWELL: The same as you're saying today.

MRS. PEACOCK: About the hippopotamus?

MRS CARTWELL & WHOLEWIG: The what?!!!

MRS. PEACOCK: Mrs. Luvadore was simply divulging the size of a hippopotamus she observed while on safari with Mr. Luvadore last spring.

MRS. LUVADORE: Yes. Why, Mrs. Peacock simply asked me to reprise the story of when I last accompanied my husband on one of his many expeditions, when we suddenly made acquaintance with a rather corpulent but well-behaved female. Don't you recall that, Mrs. Wholewig?

MRS. WHOLEWIG: *(With a gentle reluctance.)* Why, yes...I must say, I do. Don't you recall that, Mrs. Cartwell?

MRS. CARTWELL: *(Slight pause, suspiciously.)* I do...vaguely recall it.

MRS. LUVADORE: Well, there you are then.

MRS. CARTWELL: And what about yesterday?

MRS. LUVADORE: Why, what about yesterday, my dear?

MRS. CARTWELL: What were you describing as having a most "ample rump"? A camel?

MRS. PEACOCK: I believe a camel has a *hump*.

MRS. CARTWELL: Regardless, I distinctly overheard my name attached to the term "ample rump", soon after accompanied by a childish yet menacing guffaw. Why, you even included the waiter.

MRS. LUVADORE: "Ample rump"?

199

MRS. CARTWELL: Yes.

MRS. LUVADORE: What could I have said yesterday that included the term "ample rump"? Do you recall, Mrs. Peacock?

MRS. PEACOCK: Why, I haven't a clue. Ample rump?

MRS. CARTWELL: Indeed.

(As LUVADORE and PEACOCK repeat "Ample rump" in hushed tones throughout the following, in an attempt to recall...)

MRS. WHOLEWIG: My dear, perhaps this was another slight misunderstanding, not unlike today.

MRS. CARTWELL: I am not delusional. I know what I overheard.

MRS. WHOLEWIG: However, it does appear that neither of them can honestly recall...

MRS. CARTWELL: Oh, don't go by their quizzical façade. They have always worked in tandem, so why should now be any different?

MRS. WHOLEWIG: But a duel, of all things? How can you make such a threat?

MRS. CARTWELL: How can't I?

MRS. WHOLEWIG: But you're a lady. Ladies don't handle weapons.

MRS. CARTWELL: Well, maybe they should start. *(Suddenly, to Luvadore & Peacock...)* **Will you stop repeating that phrase, please?!!!**

MRS. LUVADORE & PEACOCK: *(A lightbulb!)* I remember now!

MRS. CARTWELL: Oh, do you.

MRS. LUVADORE: Shortly after you had departed, our waiter approached us with 3 complimentary teacakes, intended to be sampled by the three of us, due to the absence of Mrs. Wholewig.

MRS. PEACOCK: We then inquired as to the flavor, as it was somewhat unusual for teacake.

MRS. LUVADORE: Our waiter then provided that it was - *Apple Rum.*

MRS. PEACOCK: To which we conveyed that it was unfortunate that you were not here to sample it.

MRS. LUVADORE: To which I divulged, *"Less Apple Rum for Mrs. Cartwell means more for us".*

MRS. PEACOCK: Prompting us all to laugh, our waiter included, in the childish manner in which you observed.

> *(LUVADORE, PEACOCK and WHOLEWIG laugh in a*
> *similar way, leaving CARTWELL unsettled.)*

MRS. LUVADORE: But I can assure you, Mrs. Cartwell, that I would never utter such an insult, behind you or in front of you. Why, I've never even noticed your backside enough to make any sort of description.

MRS. PEACOCK: Nor I.

MRS. WHOLEWIG: Very well. So, if nothing else, we've established that this has all been a simple misunderstanding, yes?

MRS. PEACOCK: Well, I would certainly hope so. I always look forward to our little gatherings so much.

MRS. LUVADORE: I as well.

MRS. WHOLEWIG: Indeed.

(A moment. All observe the now humbled Mrs. Cartwell.)

MRS. CARTWELL: Yes, well...I'm afraid, at the very least, I should...apologize to both of you for my unfounded accusation. To the absurd extent of challenging you to a duel, Mrs. Luvadore,...as if I were even remotely versed in the handling of weaponry. That aside,... I suppose there is something to be said for the mind playing tricks on one's ears, and...I suppose I've said it. Much to my shame. *(A beat.)* Having said that, I kindly ask that you excuse me.

MRS. WHOLEWIG: But why, my dear?

MRS. LUVADORE: We had such succulent repartee in order for today.

MRS. CARTWELL: *(Slight pause, a great admission.)* I'm certain you do. However,...with all due respect, I believe this experience has shed light on the superficiality of it all. The energy I've invested in vanity and childlike belittlement of others, from which we've all sought similar gratification.   Why, I would go so far as to say that this misunderstanding has brought my own insecurities to the surface, which have heretofore manifested into disparaging remarks about this one's abnormally large nose or that one's torrid affair with the gardener.

MRS. PEACOCK: Whose gardener would that be?

MRS. CARTWELL: The point I'm making, Mrs. Peacock, is that it is of little significance.

And, by God, who cares if I, in fact, *do* have an *"ample rump"*? *(Slight pause, with profound liberation.)* There must be more to this life,…and I hereby vow to channel my energies into discovering what that is,…at last.

(A moment, before she starts off…)

MRS. WHOLEWIG: *(Moved by this.)* You're an inspiration, my dear.

MRS. PEACOCK: *(Moved, as she rises.)* Why, I believe you've become the first Buddhist I've ever encountered.

MRS. LUVADORE: *(Attempting to outpraise, she slowly rises.)* I too am impressed, Mrs. Cartwell. You are undoubted proof that with age comes wisdom.

MRS. CARTWELL: *(A beat, turns, intensely.)* With "age"?

PEACOCK & WHOLEWIG: *(Looking at Luvadore fearfully.)* Oh, dear.

(The lights go out.)

End of Play

DID YOU HEAR THE ONE ABOUT THE MEXICAN LAUNDRESS?

DID YOU HEAR THE ONE ABOUT
THE MEXICAN LAUNDRESS?

Did You Hear the One About the Mexican Laundress? received
its NYC Premiere as part of Howling Moon Cab Company's
Arcs and Triumphs Festival in April-May 2008
at Where Eagles Dare Theatre in New York City,
with the following cast and director:

FLORA.....................Judy Alvarez
ARVIN....................Andrew Dahl
BAILEY..............Nicholas Daniele

Directed by the Author

Artistic Directors: Jonathan and Meri Wallace

Did You Hear the One About the Mexican Laundress?
received its World Premier as part of Teatro del Pueblo's
6th Annual Political Theatre Festival in February 2007,
in St. Paul, MN.

Cast of Characters

FLORA - *Late 40's-50's. A suspect. Mexican born. Mexican accent. Wears a bandana and traditional Mexican dress.*

ARVIN - *Mid-to-late 30's. Male, a federal agent. Caucasian. Wears a white dress shirt, black slacks, black tie & sunglasses.*

BAILEY - *Mid-to-late 30's. Male, a federal agent. Caucasian. Wears a white dress shirt, black slacks, black tie & sunglasses.*

A questioning room.

The Time – 2004.

Technical Note: The "two-way mirror" is the audience (down-stage).

DID YOU HEAR THE ONE ABOUT
THE MEXICAN LAUNDRESS?

*(FLORA sits behind table, in between ARVIN, with one foot up-
on chair, and BAILEY, standing.)*

*(A considerable moment, as ARVIN & BAILEY gaze intensely at
FLORA, who observes them quizzically and with building
impatience...before...)*

FLORA: What?

ARVIN: We'll wait.

FLORA: For what?

ARVIN: You know.

FLORA: Know what? I told you, I don't know what the hell's
going on here? What is dis?

BAILEY: Please lower your voice.

FLORA: Or what? You'll kidnap me? You already did that.

ARVIN: Mam, you haven't been kidnapped.

FLORA: No? Y'don't call it kidnapping when you take someone off da' street and throw dem into a car and don't tell dem
why? What the hell do you call it den?

ARVIN: Mam, we'll ask the questions here, alright?

BAILEY: You have not been kidnapped. This is all perfectly
legal.

FLORA: Legal in whose mind?

ARVIN: Ms. Dominguez, we are with the Federal Bureau of
Investigations.

FLORA: Yeah, so what's the difference between you and any loco who abducts someone? The sunglasses?

ARVIN: Mam, we'll ask the questions here, alright?

BAILEY: Ms. Dominguez, we are government representatives.

FLORA: Hey, I know what the FBI is, okay? I wasn't born yesterday. And what I **also** know is dat you can't just take an innocent citizen into custody without a reason.

BAILEY: We have a reason.

FLORA: And what reason is dat?

BAILEY: Our suspicion.

FLORA: What suspicion?

ARVIN: We have reasonable suspicion.

FLORA: *"Reasonable suspicion?"*

BAILEY: That's right.

FLORA: What the hell are you suspicious of?

ARVIN: Ms. Dominguez, we'll ask the questions here, alright?

FLORA: You guys haven't asked a question. You've just brought me here and stared at me like I'm an armadillo with a goat head. You want an answer den ask a question.

(A moment, as BAILEY & ARVIN look at each other before removing their sunglasses in sync, and pursuing with enhanced intensity...)

BAILEY: Ms. Dominguez, you're not American born, are you?

DID YOU HEAR THE ONE ABOUT
THE MEXICAN LAUNDRESS?

FLORA: What gave it away?

ARVIN; So the answer is "No".

FLORA: Yes.

BAILEY: Yes the answer is "No"?

FLORA: Yes.

ARVIN: Alright. So why are you here?

FLORA: Why are *you*?

BAILEY: Ms. Dominguez, we'll ask the questions here, alright?

FLORA: Alright, fine. I'm here because I wanted to come here.

ARVIN: You wanted to come here.

FLORA: Yes. And I did. *Legally.*

ARVIN: And from where did you come?

FLORA: Mexico.

ARVIN: Are you sure?

FLORA: Am I sure? Yes, I'm sure. How can I not be sure where I'm from?

BAILEY: Ms. Dominguez, we'll ask the questions here, alright?

FLORA: Yes, I'm sure where I'm from.

ARVIN: Do you like this country?

FLORA: I *love* this country.

BAILEY: Do you have any axes to grind with this country or its government.

FLORA: *"Axes to grind"*? No, I don't have any "axes to grind".

ARVIN: You don't resent it?

FLORA: Absolutely not.

BAILEY: You hate this country, don't you?

FLORA: What?! I jus' told you I love this country. This country has given me great opportunity.

BAILEY: Oh, well, I'm sure it has.

FLORA: What the hell does *dat* mean?

ARVIN: Ms. Dominguez, we'll ask the questions here, alright?

BAILEY: Do you have certain...*religious* allegiances?

FLORA: What?

ARVIN: Do you espouse Islamic beliefs?

FLORA: Espouse *what*?

BAILEY: Are you a Muslim?

FLORA: Muslim? Have you ever heard of a Mexican Muslim?

ARVIN: Yes, we have.

DID YOU HEAR THE ONE ABOUT
THE MEXICAN LAUNDRESS?

FLORA: Well, I'm not, okay?

BAILEY: Then maybe you're not really Mexican either.

FLORA: What the hell are you talking about?

ARVIN: Why should we believe you're a Mexican and not a Muslim?

FLORA: Because I told you, that's why. What is this, *Jeopardy for Dummies*? What the hell are you asking me dese questions for?

BAILEY: Regardless of *why* we're asking you this, you are required to answer.

FLORA: Says who?

ARVIN: Says the United States Government.

FLORA: Let me tell you what the United States government requires me to do; the United States Government requires me to pay my taxes and don't break the law, okay?

BAILEY: You were seen transporting a powdered substance which is suspected of being a chemical used in making explosives, and *that*, Ms. Dominguez, *is* breaking the law.

FLORA: Are you for real?

ARVIN: Oh, we're quite real, Ms. Dominguez.

FLORA: And who witnessed dis?

BAILEY: Who witnessed what?

FLORA: Who saw me transport dis substance?

ARVIN: We did.

FLORA: You did.

BAILEY: That's right.

FLORA: *(Slight Pause.)* So you're *"reasonable suspicion"* is that I am a *terrorist?*

ARVIN: You said it. We didn't.

BAILEY: We're saying that we have reason to suspect that you had intentions of committing or partaking in the commitment of an illegal activity.

FLORA: Which is making a bomb?

BAILEY: You said it. We didn't.

ARVIN: Look, you're in our custody now, mam, so you may as well put your cards out.

FLORA: Put my cards out?

BAILEY: Show your hand.

FLORA: Show my hand?

ARVIN: Come clean.

BAILEY: CONFESS!

FLORA: What the hell are you guys trying to do?! You think you can drag any dark-haired person off the street and bully them into admitting something dey don't even know how to do because you can talk like Dragnet?!

ARVIN: Mam, that's enough.

FLORA: Don't you tell *me* what's enough. I don't know anything about making explosives.

ARVIN: Well, we think you may.

BAILEY: Or we think you may know someone who does.

ARVIN: Either way, Ms. Dominguez, you have given us *reasonable suspicion.*

FLORA: In other words, you think I'm in cahoots with Bin Laden because I don't look like Clay Aiken.

BAILEY: Mam, we'll ask the questions here, alright?

FLORA: I wasn't asking a question. Dat was a statement.

ARVIN: We'll also make the statements.

FLORA: How can I answer your questions if only *you* can make the statements?

BAILEY: Mam, we'll ask the questions here, alright?!!!

ARVIN: *(Defensively...)* You can only make a statement in response to our questions, alright?!!!

BAILEY: *(Hostilely...)* What were you planning to use that substance for?!!!

FLORA: What substance?!

ARVIN: Mam, we'll ask the questions here, alright?

BAILEY: It was in your possession when we picked you up.

ARVIN: It was in the trunk of your car.

213

BAILEY: What were you doing with it?!!!

FLORA: What was I doing with **detergent**?!

BAILEY: If that's what you wana' call it.

FLORA: It's not what I want to call it. It's what it *is*.

ARVIN: Then why were you transporting so much of it?

FLORA: Whata' you think cleans clothes, Miracle Whip? You need detergent for that.

BAILEY: 200 lbs of it?

FLORA: Yes.

ARVIN: That's an awful lot of detergent for one woman.

FLORA: What, are you kidding? It's not for me. It's for my business.

ARVIN: Oh, your *"business"*.

BAILEY: Here we go.

ARVIN: And what *"business"* is that, Ms. **Do-min-gueeeeeeeeez?**

FLORA: *(Slight pause, resentfully.)* I'm a laundress.

BAILEY: *(Got 'er.)* HE-LLO!

FLORA: What *"hello"*? I own a Laundromat in Astoria, Queens.

ARVIN: Look at that. She *heads* the operation.

FLORA: What operation?

BAILEY: The **money-laundering** operation.

FLORA: *Money-laundering*?!

ARVIN & BAILEY: You said it. We didn't.

FLORA: I didn't say I laundered money. I don't even know what money laundering is. I run a legitimate business.

ARVIN: Oh, we're sure you do.

BAILEY: As a front.

FLORA: A what?

ARVIN: A front.

FLORA: A front for what?

BAILEY: Your *real* business.

ARVIN: Cocaine?!

BAILEY: Opium?!

ARVIN: **Heroin?!!!**

FLORA: *(Slight pause.)* Wait a second. Are you guys accusing me of being a terrorist, a money launderer or a drug dealer?

*(BAILEY & ARVIN look at each other, perplexed...
A beat.)*

BAILEY: Well,...um...I...well....

ARVIN: Look, we're asking the questions here, alright?!!!

FLORA: *(As she rises...)* Yeah, well, from now on you can ask the two-way mirror because I ain't answering anymore questions. Estoy cansado de esta mierda! **And I want your names!**

ARVIN: Mam,...

FLORA: I want your names right now! I am a legal citizen and my rights have been violated!

ARVIN: Ms. Dominguez, your rights have been revoked!

FLORA: What the hell do you mean my rights have been *revoked*?! Have you ever read the Constitution?!

BAILEY: Have **you** ever read the Patriot Act?!

FLORA: No, have **YOU**?!!!!

*(BAILEY and ARVIN look at each other, perplexed...
A beat.)*

BAILEY: Well,...

ARVIN: Um...

BAILEY: No, actually...

ARVIN: Regardless, we've been told that we can conduct "random searches and seizures"!

FLORA: Really?

BAILEY: Yes.

FLORA: Searches and seizures.

ARVIN: That's right.

FLORA: Well, I tell you what, why don't you go out and search for someone who is actually guilty of something and then go into convulsions, okay? There's your Search and your Seizure. Alright? Now I want your names.

BAILEY & ARVIN: Mam,...

FLORA: I am not answering anymore of your insulting questions, do you comprende?! My business has lost a day's worth of income thanks to you. *(Angrily sits!)* **Now give me a pen and paper!!!**

(An odd, considerable moment between BAILEY & ARVIN, who look at each other, ...then out..., before BAILEY timidly extends a small pad, which FLORA bitterly swipes. Awaiting a pen, she soon turns to ARVIN who, similar to BAILEY, extends pen tentatively, which she, again, hostilely swipes.)

(With BAILEY and ARVIN on either side of FLORA, facing out like two momentarily humbled pillars...)

FLORA: Your name?

(A beat, as ARVIN & BAILEY look at each other, uneasily...)

HE-LLO! Your name?

ARVIN: *(Murmurs, begrudgingly...)* Agent Arvin.

FLORA: Orange?!

ARVIN: *(Slightly louder.)* Arvin.

217

FLORA: Spell it.

ARVIN: A-R-V-I-N.

FLORA: And yours?

BAILEY: *(A beat, before...)* Agent Bailey.

FLORA: B-A-I-L-E-Y?

BAILEY: *(Murmurs...)* Yes.

FLORA: What?!

BAILEY: *(Reluctantly louder...)* Yes.

FLORA: Agent Arvin and Agent Bailey. What a coincidence. Both your mommies gave you the same first name.

(FLORA slams pen on table, rises...)

ARVIN: *(With bogus authority.)* Mam, we're not through with you.

FLORA: Oh, you better believe you're not through with **me**.

BAILEY: Mam, you are still considered a suspect!

FLORA: A suspect of *what*?!

(BAILEY & ARVIN look at each other...)

BAILEY: *(A beat.)* Of...

ARVIN: *(A beat.)* ...something?

FLORA: You know, I think you might be the stupidest gringos I have ever been abducted by.

DID YOU HEAR THE ONE ABOUT
THE MEXICAN LAUNDRESS?

(FLORA motions to door…)

ARVIN: Mam,…

FLORA: "Mam" nothing! **And where the hell is my deter-gent?!**

BAILEY: It's…it's being examined.

FLORA: Examined?

ARVIN: It's…it's in a lab. They're inspecting it.

FLORA: They're *inspecting* it?! All the tax dollars people pay for you geniuses to abduct little Mexican women and examine 200 pounds of *Tide*?!!!

BAILEY: Ms. Dominguez, you're…

(…as FLORA angrily moves down center, to the two-way mirror…)

FLORA: Let me tell you, if I walk in that lab and those idiotas are washing their socks with my detergent, heads will roll! And as for you, Barnum and Bailey…

ARVIN: *(With tepid assertion.)* Arvin…and Bailey.

FLORA: Who gives a shit?! It's the same circus with different clowns. You boys'd be better off learning to juggle anyway. At least you'd be amusing people intentionally.

(FLORA motions to door, but is currently blocked by BAILEY and ARVIN, who stand side-by-side.)

(An intense moment, akin to a Mexican standoff, before FLORA gives an authoritative throat-clearing.)

219

*(Another moment,...before BAILEY and ARVIN
swing open ever slowly and humbly, like a human
double door. FLORA motions to the actual door,
then stops...)*

You'll be hearing from my lawyer.

(FLORA exits, slams door!)

(BAILEY and ARVIN are still, and sufficiently emasculated.)

*(A moment. They awkwardly amble towards table, as if
attempting to mask their humiliation.)*

(A moment.)

ARVIN: Um...should we have just let her leave like that?

BAILEY: Um...I...probably not, but...she seemed a little upset.

ARVIN: Yeah. *(Slight pause.)* It's much easier when they're
afraid.

*(A beat, before they turn out slowly and sheepishly, facing
the two-way mirror which now watches them...)*

(The lights go out.)

End of Play

Daniel Damiano is an Award-winning Playwright, Actor, Screenwriter, Poet and Novelist based in Brooklyn, NY. His plays have been performed throughout many areas of the U.S., as well as London, England and Sydney & Melbourne, Australia. His acclaimed play DAY OF THE DOG premiered with St. Louis Actors' Studio in 2013 and subsequently transferred to 59E59 in NYC in 2014. It was a 2013 St. Louis Critics Choice Best Play Nominee, and is published by Broadway Play Publishing. His play THE WILD BOAR was a 2022 Finalist for Dayton Playhouse's Futurefest, as well as a previous Finalist for both the Woodward/Newman Drama Award and the Janet & Bruce Bunch Award. He has been awarded the 2024 David A. Einhorn Playwriting Prize (for *The Desser Cart*) and the Christopher Brian Wolk Award for Playwriting (for *Dreams of Friendly Aliens*). He was a 2013 Nominee for the Pushcart Poetry Prize and a Finalist for the 2012 Arts & Letters Prize for Drama. His three novels THE WOMAN IN THE SUN HAT *(2021, Seattle Book Review Recommendation)*, GRAPHIC NATURE (2022) and ADVICE FROM A CAT (2024) have all been published by fandango 4 Art House. His two books of poetry are 104 DAYS OF THE PANDEMIC (2021, fandango 4 Art House) and THE CONCRETE JUNGLE AND THE SURROUNDING AREAS (2024, Bottlecap Press). His poetry has been published in the MacGuffin, Gyroscope Review, Philly Poetry Chapbook Review, Curlew Quarterly, Quagmire Magazine, Crooked Teeth Literary Magazine, Newtown Literary Journal, Cloudbank, New Voices Anthology and HotMetal Press.

MESSAGE TO ACTORS & PRODUCERS:

Actors are welcome to use excerpts from these plays for the purposes of acting and scene-study classes as well as auditions, but it is *strongly* requested that the author's name and play title be clearly noted.

Theatre producers, if there is interest in any of these works for public performance, please reach out to the publisher of this collection, fandango 4 Art House, or to the Playwright directly.

We at fandango 4 Art House also welcome all readers to share their reviews, most notably on its Goodreads and/or Amazon pages, and welcome recommendations to local bookstores.

Thank you.

***

Other Published Works by Daniel Damiano

DAY OF THE DOG (Play)
(Broadway Play Publishing)

THE WOMAN IN THE SUN HAT (Novel)
(fandango 4 Art House)

104 DAYS OF THE PANDEMIC (Poetry)
(fandango 4 Art House)

THE GIFT OF WHAT FOR (Short Story)
Palm Circle Press Short Story Anthology 2021
(Palm Circle Press)

GRAPHIC NATURE (Novel)
(fandango 4 Art House)

PLAYS BY DANIEL DAMIANO Vol 1
(fandango 4 Art House)

ADVICE FROM A CAT (Novel)
(fandango 4 Art House)

THE CONCRETE JUNGLE
AND THE SURROUNDING AREAS (Poems)
(Bottlecap Press)